Voices of Baseball

Bob Chieger

VOICES OF BASEBALL

Quotations on the

Summer Game

ATHENEUM NEW YORK 1983

LIBRARY OF CONGRESS CATALOGING IN PUBLICATION DATA

Chieger, Bob.
Voices of baseball.

Bibliography: p.
Includes index.
1. Baseball—Quotations, maxims, etc. I. Title.
GV867.3.C47   1983   796.357   82-73027
ISBN 0-689-70646-4

Copyright © 1983 by Bob Chieger
All rights reserved
Published simultaneously in Canada by McClelland and Stewart Ltd.
Composed by Maryland Linotype Composition Company,
    Baltimore, Maryland
Manufactured by Fairfield Graphics, Fairfield, Pennsylvania
Designed by Mary Cregan
First Printing March 1983
Second Printing May 1983

All afternoon, there was the ceaseless, murmuring undercurrent of people talking and exclaiming—people taking in a game. These were the voices of baseball I like best of all.

Roger Angell
***The New Yorker*, 1978**

Contents

Introduction

1.	Baseball	3
2.	Baseball and Other Sports	8
3.	Baserunning	11
4.	Blacks, Whites, and Browns	13
5.	Brains and Flakes	16
6.	Catching	21
7.	Cities and Teams	24
8.	Coaches and Scouts	45
9.	Drinking and Debauchery	47
10.	Equipment	52
11.	Exercise, Diet, and Injuries	54
12.	Famous Last Words	58
13.	Fans	61
14.	Fielding	67
15.	Hitting and Missing	71
16.	Home Runs	77
17.	Infielders	81
18.	Labor	97
19.	Leisure and Travel	100
20.	Macho	103
21.	Managing	105

22. Minor Leagues 117
23. Modern/Olden Days 121
24. Money 125
25. Outfielders 130
26. Owners and Executives 146
27. Philosophy 153
28. Pitching 157
29. Politics and Baseball 178
30. Records, Awards, and Statistics 182
31. Rookies and Veterans 185
32. Spitters and Beanballs 189
33. Sportswriters 194
34. Spring Training 198
35. Television and Radio 201
36. Umpires 206
37. Utility Players and Trades 211
38. Winning and Losing 215
39. Wives and Family 218
40. World Series 221

Bibliography 229
Index 235

Introduction

If you are a baseball fan like me, you might realize that you spend more time reading and talking about baseball than you spend attending the games.

Baseball, it has been said, affords the opportunity for the generations to talk with one another. To that I can testify: While some people have difficulty talking to their parents, this fan can go on for hours with his mother about her adopted son, Billy Martin, and his Oakland A's. Mother even chose her young hairdresser because of her knowledge of the game. In the 1950s, my grandfather would stay tuned to his Philco console radio, listening to Ernie Harwell and George Kell describe the antics of his beloved Detroit Tigers. When we visited every Sunday, the first thing he said when we came through the door was "Damn Tigers!" Often, that was the only thing he said all day. Some teams lend themselves more to conversation than others.

Why are there so many wise and witty sayings pertaining to baseball? Jim Bouton, one of baseball's many philosophers, says that because of the slow pace of the game, every ballplayer and fan is a storyteller. "How many basketball or football stories have you heard?" asks Bouton. "There might be a few—but there are *hundreds* of baseball stories."

I found Bouton's point to be true as I pursued a lifelong habit of collecting quotations. Of the six hundred subjects under which I categorized the tens of thousands of quotes I collected on index cards, four had many more quotations than the others: love, sex, death, and—of course—baseball. When it was suggested that I pick one subject for a book of quotations, the subject was easy to choose. I love baseball, and I have spent more time playing it and reading about it and know more about it than the other three subjects combined.

You almost cannot avoid the baseball sayings that have entered our culture. How many times has someone said to you, "It's not over 'till it's over"—a favorite saying of Yogi Berra's. Or used Ring Lardner's baseball phrase, popularized by Casey Stengel: "You could look it up." Lardner's saying is so prevalent that you suspect you really *can* look everything up, as though there is a huge data bank somewhere where *everything* you want to know can be found easily. If only everything were as scrupulously reported on and recorded as baseball.

This book attempts to add yet another brick to the castle of baseball lore and information, another place where us fans could look it up: a book that is meant to be read not only for enjoyment, but to provide historical information on important quotations for serious students of the game.

I think it is rather odd that whereas a sport such as football will tend to wash over us, almost every baseball fan is a student of the game. Although I can't remember who won last year's Super Bowl, I can still remember where I was when Don Larsen pitched the perfect game, when Bill Mazeroski hit the "shot heard 'round the world," or when Herb Score was hit in the eye by Gil McDougald's batted ball. In those three examples mentioned, I was (1) on an extended school recess in order to listen in, (2) missing class by watching the game in the school library, and (3) listening by transistor radio in the back of the class via an earphone taped to my wrist.

Although this would argue for a misspent youth, watching

a bunch of folks on a sunny afternoon hitting and throwing balls while another group of people sit watching, fills me with delight even today. The world is roaring by on its serious, involved course, but here are some people who have suspended time and are just enjoying themselves. And to think that in the major leagues alone, there are over two thousand of these mini-Woodstocks taking place across the country from spring until fall.

And before, after, and even during the contest, not only are the fans chatting about the game, but so are the players. Baseball allows that space. The only thing I ever hear during a frantic basketball game is the coach yelling, "No foul! No foul!" But take Pete Rose, after a runner crashed into him at third running out a triple. Oddly, the runner who was on first at the time failed to score, because he tripped coming home. Rose dusted himself off and said to the guy who clubbed the triple, "How come you didn't knock his ass in?"

This book, I hope, will capture the flavor of the summer game. When I was young, I used to think the Hot Stove League was a group of old geezers who met regularly in a wooden shack with a pot-bellied stove to swap lies and stories about baseball. I always wanted to join.

So this book is dedicated to the players and fans as a contribution to that mythical Hot Stove League, for those of us who enjoy playing the sport in the "inner game" of the mind as well as on the field.

Bob Chieger
Los Gatos, California
February 1983

Voices of Baseball

Chapter 1

Baseball

A sensational event was changing from the brown suit to the gray contents of his pockets. He was earnest about these objects. They were of eternal importance, like baseball or the Republican Party. **Sinclair Lewis,** *Babbitt,* **1922**

There ain't much to being a ballplayer—if you're a ballplayer.
Honus Wagner, former infielder, 1949

Baseball becomes dull only to those with dull minds. Today's game is always different from yesterday's game.
Red Smith, *New York Herald-Tribune*

Baseball is a kind of collective chess with arms and legs in full play under sunlight.
Jacques Barzun, *God's Country and Mine,* **1954**

In baseball, you don't know *nothing.*
Yogi Berra, New York Yankees catcher

To be good, you've gotta have a lot of little boy in you. When you see Willie Mays and Ted Williams jumping and hopping around the bases after hitting a home run, and the kissing and hugging that goes on at home plate, you realize they have to be little boys.
Roy Campanella, Brooklyn Dodgers catcher, 1957

Baseball is a lot like life. The line drives are caught, the squibbers go for base hits. It's an unfair game.
Rod Kanehl, New York Mets infielder, 1963

Only in baseball can a team player be a pure individualist first and a team player second, within the rules and the spirit of the game. **Branch Rickey, *The American Diamond*, 1965**

No game in the world is as tidy and dramatically neat as baseball, with cause and effect, crime and punishment, motive and result, so cleanly defined. **Paul Gallico, sportswriter**

Baseball is a game which consists of tapping a ball with a piece of wood, then running like a lunatic. **H. J. Dutiel, writer**

I'm just happy to be here. I'll take whatever they give me. If they took off my hat and shit in it, I'd put it right back on my head and say thanks.
Jerry Stephenson, Seattle Pilots pitcher, 1969

A critic once characterized baseball as six minutes of action crammed into two-and-one-half hours.
Ray Fitzgerald, *Boston Globe*, 1970

Since baseball time is measured only in outs, all you have to do is succeed utterly; keep hitting, keep the rally alive, and you have defeated time. You remain forever young.
Roger Angell, *The Summer Game*, 1972

There are only five things you can do in baseball—run, throw, catch, hit, and hit with power.
Leo Durocher, Houston Astros manager, 1973

Abner Doubleday didn't invent baseball. Baseball invented Abner Doubleday.

Harold Peterson, *The Man Who Invented Baseball,* **1973**

The reason I love baseball so much is because when I come into a game in the bottom of the ninth, bases loaded, no one out and a one-run lead . . . it takes people off my mind.

Tug McGraw, *Screwball,* **1974**

To enjoy baseball, you do not need violence in your heart.

Charles Einstein, sportswriter

It is designed to break your heart. The game begins in the spring, when everything else begins again, and it blossoms in the summer, filling the afternoons and evenings, and then as soon as the chill rains come, it stops and leaves you to face the fall alone.

A. Bartlett Giamatti, "The Green Fields of the Mind," 1975

The whole history of baseball has the quality of mythology.

Bernard Malamud, novelist

In the country of baseball, time is the air we breathe, and the wind swirls us backward and forward, until we seem so reckoned in time and seasons that all time and all seasons become the same.

Donald Hall, *In the Country of Baseball,* **1976**

Baseball is beautiful . . . the supreme performing art. It combines in perfect harmony the magnificient features of ballet, drama, art, and ingenuity.

Bowie Kuhn, commissioner of baseball, 1976

Baseball has stood for loyalty to the verities, memories of innocence, patience with ritual; surely no one who cared about baseball could be an opportunist at heart.

Edward Hoagland, "A Fan's Notes," 1977

More than other games, baseball gives its players space—
both physical and emotional—in which to define themselves.
John Eskow, *New Times,* **1978**

The first big-league game I ever saw was at the Polo Grounds.
My father took me. I remember it so well—the green grass
and the green stands. It was like seeing Oz.
John Curtis, San Francisco Giants pitcher, 1978

I don't think you *can* think too hard. Baseball, when you really
analyze it, is a game within a game within a game.
Skip Lockwood, New York Mets pitcher, 1978

Baseball is the favorite American sport because it's so slow.
Any idiot can follow it. And just about any idiot can play it.
Gene Vidal, father of Gore Vidal,
in Gore's book *Matters of Fact and Fiction,* **1979**

The umpires always say "Play ball." They don't say "Work
ball." **Willie Stargell, Pittsburgh Pirates infielder, 1979**

Baseball endures at least in part because it is a contemplative
sport that delights in its nuances. Not a brazen game, eager to
sell its thrills cheaply, but rather an understated affair that
must be courted if it's to be loved.
Kenneth Turan, "It's a Grand Old Game," 1979

The clock doesn't matter in baseball. Time stands still or
moves backward. Theoretically, one game could go on forever. Some seem to.
Herb Caen, *San Francisco Chronicle,* **1979**

Baseball is taking life ninety feet at a time.
Roger Rosenblatt, "Special Edition," PBS-TV, 1979

Baseball is a kid's game that grownups only tend to screw up.
Bob Lemon, New York Yankees manager, 1979

Baseball is not precisely a team sport. It is more a series of concerts by the artists.   **Jim Murray, *Los Angeles Times*, 1979**

Baseball is very much like life. Watch it closely, and you will learn a great deal about things like courage, beauty, strength, finesse, chance, fallibility, and loyalty. Study baseball and you will have a head start in understanding life.
Jim Langford, *The Game Is Never Over*, 1980

More than any other American sport, baseball creates the magnetic, addictive illusion that it can almost be understood.
Thomas Boswell, *Inside Sports*, 1980

Only 650 of us can be at the top at any one time. That's how many players are in the bigs. The rest of us, we might be doctors and lawyers and Indian chiefs—but as long as we're not outfielders for the Indians, we're failures.
Leonard Shapiro, *Inside Sports*, 1980

I ain't ever had a job. I just always played baseball.
Satchel Paige, former pitcher, 1980

I've always had the feeling of being invulnerable on a diamond—that nothing really bad could happen to me within those lines.   **Richard Grossinger, writer, 1980**

I'm from the generation that forgives baseball everything.
Pete Hamill, New York *Daily News*, 1981

Anytime you think you have the game conquered, the game will turn around and punch you right in the nose.
Mike Schmidt, Philadelphia Phillies infielder, 1981

Baseball and malaria keep coming back.
Gene Mauch, California Angels manager, 1982

Chapter 2

Baseball and
Other Sports

Baseball has the great advantage over cricket of being sooner ended. **George Bernard Shaw, writer**

The rigid voluntary rules of right and wrong, as applied in American sports, are second only to religion in strengthening the morals of the American people . . . and baseball is the greatest of all team sports. **Herbert C. Hoover**

What do you want, a bonus or a limp?
**Fresco Thompson, Los Angeles Dodgers executive,
persuading a prospect to choose baseball over football**

You can't sit on a lead and run a few plays into the line and just kill the clock. You've got to throw the ball over the goddamn plate and give the other man his chance. That's why baseball is the greatest game of them all.
Earl Weaver, Baltimore Orioles manager, 1969

Football is technological, baseball is pastoral. Football is played in a stadium, baseball is played in a park. Football is played on an enclosed grid. . . . Baseball is played on an ever-widening field with boundaries that reach to infinity.

George Carlin,
"An Evening with Wally Londo" (record), 1974

In football the object is to march into enemy territory and cross his goal. In baseball the object is to go home.   George Carlin

Baseball is the only game left for people. To play basketball now, you have to be seven-foot-six. To play football you have to be the same width.

Bill Veeck, Chicago White Sox owner, 1975

Baseball happens to be a game of cumulative tension. . . . Football, basketball and hockey are played with hand grenades and machine guns.

John Leonard, *The New York Times*, 1975

Baseball is easy to fathom, not like football, which people explain to me at great length and I understand for one brief moment before it all falls apart in my brain and looks like an ominous calculus problem.

Eve Babitz, "Dodger Stadium," 1977

Football may be the "disco beat" of modern sports, but baseball is Chopin or the mystique of Mozart. Every baseball game is new with the pristine beauty of the notes of Beethoven's Ninth.   Philip Gerstle, *San Francisco Examiner*, 1979

It is the sport that a foreigner is least likely to take to. You have to grow up playing it, you have to accept the lore of the bubble-gum card, and believe that if the answer to the Mays-Snider-Mantle question is found, then the universe will be a simpler and more ordered place.

David Halberstam, writer, 1979

The other sports are just sports. Baseball is a love.

Bryant Gumbel, sportscaster, 1981

Baseball is a story that weaves itself through every single day of its season. In football you watch the game on Sunday, and that's it. I'm not interested in how a guy hits the tackling dummy on Wednesday. **Al Michaels, sportscaster, 1981**

No other sporting event can compare with a good Series. The Super Bowl is a three-hour interruption in a week of drink and Rotarian parties. **Roger Kahn,** *Sport,* **1981**

Do they have any knucklebowlers?
**Lindsey Nelson, San Francisco Giants announcer,
asking a colleague about cricket, 1981**

The difference between soccer and baseball is that in baseball you have a father taking his son and explaining the strategy, and in soccer you have the son taking his father and explaining it to him. **Danny Villaneuva, soccer-team owner, 1981**

Our other team sports are hot-blooded, sweaty and continuous. . . . Only baseball is cold-blooded and discontinuous. The game explodes at unpredictable instants. You start to sweat *after* the play is over.
Thomas Boswell, *How Life Imitates the World Series,* **1982**

The larger the ball, the less the writing about the sport. There are superb books about golf, very good books about baseball, not many good books about football, and very few good books about basketball. There are no books about beachballs.
George Plimpton, writer, 1982

Chapter 3

Baserunning

The whole secret of sliding is to make your move at the last possible second. When I went in there I wanted to see the whites of the fielder's eyes.   **Ty Cobb, Detroit Tigers outfielder**

He was thrown out trying to steal second; his head was full of larceny but his feet were honest.

**Arthur "Bugs" Baer,
sportswriter, on outfielder Ping Bodie, 1917**

I couldn't. I carry my cigars in my back pocket and I was afraid I'd break them.

**Jimmy Dykes, Philadelphia Athletics infielder,
when asked why he didn't slide**

He runs too long in one place. He's gotta lot of up 'n' down, but not much forward.

Dizzy Dean, St. Louis Cardinals pitcher, on a teammate

I thought they'd stop the game and give me second base.

**Milt May, Houston Astros catcher,
on stealing the first base in his six-year career, 1975**

First base is nowhere.   **Lou Brock, *Stealing Is My Game*, 1976**

When we played softball, I'd steal second, then feel guilty and go back.   **Woody Allen**

The ball jumps off the bat and you're running to first, drifting outside the line to start you on your way to second. The ultimate pleasure in baseball is that abstract moment when everything comes together and flows naturally.
Ted Simmons, St. Louis Cardinals catcher

When he runs, it's all downhill.
**Vin Scully, Los Angeles Dodgers announcer,
on Maury Wills**

There was nothing to lose.
**Ron Fairly, California Angels infielder,
asked if he had lost any speed, 1978**

Never trust a baserunner who's limping. Comes a base hit and you'll think he just got back from Lourdes.
Joe Garagiola, broadcaster, 1979

I had a brain spasm.
**Tim Blackwell, Chicago Cubs catcher,
when asked why he stopped between bases, 1981**

I'm convinced that every boy, in his heart, would rather steal second base than an automobile.   **Justice Tom Clark, 1981**

You stay in it for as long as you can until something happens. Then, you look for someone to run into.
**Mark Belanger, Baltimore Orioles infielder,
on how to beat a rundown, 1981**

What the Yankees need is a second-base coach.
Graig Nettles, New York Yankees infielder, 1982

Chapter 4

Blacks, Whites, and Browns

You ignorant, ill-bred foreigners! If you don't like the way I'm doing things out there, why don't you just pack up and go back to your own countries!

**Chief Bender, American Indian,
Philadelphia Athletics pitcher, to jeering fans, *c.*1910**

There is only one way you can be the first Negro to successfully break the color line—there is only one way. You can't retaliate. You can't answer a blow with a blow. You can't echo a curse with a curse.

**Branch Rickey, Brooklyn Dodgers general manager,
to Jackie Robinson, 1947**

I don't care if the guy is yellow or black, or if he has stripes like a fuckin' zebra. I'm the manager of this team, and I say he plays.

**Leo Durocher, Brooklyn Dodgers manager, to players
threatening to strike because of Jackie Robinson, 1947**

Jackie Robinson is the loneliest man I have ever seen in sports.
                              Jimmy Cannon, sportswriter, 1947

I was a member of the NAACP before it became camp.
                    Mudcat Grant, Minnesota Twins pitcher, 1965

Nixon was your President. But Martin Luther King was my President.   Willie Mays, San Francisco Giants outfielder, 1968

I remember one game I got five hits and stole five bases, but none of it was written down because they didn't bring the scorebook to the game that day.
            Cool Papa Bell, former Negro-leagues outfielder

Baseball is very big with my people. It figures. It's the only time we can get to shake a bat at a white man without starting a riot.   Dick Gregory, *From the Back of the Bus*, 1969

I don't see why you reporters keep confusing Brooks and me. Can't you see that we wear different numbers?
              Frank Robinson, black Baltimore Orioles outfielder,
                    on his white teammate Brooks Robinson, 1970

I am pleased that God made my skin black but I wish he had made it thicker.   Curt Flood, *The Way It Is*, 1971

I'm not bad. I'm no Joe Morgan, but I'm pretty good for a white guy.
                    Pete Rose, Philadelphia Phillies infielder,
                                          on his speed, 1979

This is by far my toughest year in baseball. I've been called everything but white.
              Bobby Bonds, Cleveland Indians outfielder, 1979

I made it as an outfielder and a pitcher with the Memphis Red Sox of the Negro leagues. In the middle of my first season they traded the left fielder and me to the Birmingham Black Barons for a bus.   Charley Pride, country singer, 1979

We were given lots of abuse to show us what we were getting into. Some kids folded when they were called obscene names but for me it was just like being back in the ghetto.

Eric Gregg, black umpire, on umpires' school, 1981

Chapter 5

Brains and Flakes

I ain't afraid to tell the world that it don't take school stuff
to help a fella play ball.

> **Shoeless Joe Jackson, Chicago White Sox outfielder**

Don't read, it'll hurt your eyes.

> **Rogers Hornsby, St. Louis Cardinals infielder**

Moe, I don't care how many of them college degrees you got.
They ain't learned you to hit that curveball no better than me.

> **Buck Crouse, Chicago White Sox catcher, to Moe Berg**

I think this stuff works. Every time I use it, I get a headache.
I think that means that hair is trying to break through.

> **Benny Bengough, New York Yankees catcher,**
> **on his hair-restorer, 1927**

A lot of folks that ain't saying ain't, ain't eating.

> **Dizzy Dean, broadcaster, on criticism of his diction, 1942**

I got as far in school as the Second Reader, only I didn't learn it all. **Dizzy Dean, 1952**

Don't cut my throat. I may want to do that myself later.
Casey Stengel, New York Yankees manager, to his barber

Yeah, but I notice that whenever I put them down, there's always some guys around ready to pick them up.
**Yogi Berra, New York Yankees catcher,
on getting teased about reading comic books**

If you are so smart, how come you are still in the Army?
**Casey Stengel, replying to a soldier who
wrote in complaining about Stengel's moves**

You'd better make it fours. I don't think I can eat six pieces.
**Yogi Berra, when asked if he wanted
his pizza cut in four or six pieces**

I don't know. I'm not in shape yet.
Yogi Berra, when asked about his cap size

Baseball is ninety percent mental. The other half is physical.
Yogi Berra

I still think neckties are designed to get in your soup.
Ted Williams, *My Turn at Bat*, 1969

Doubleheader tomorrow, barring nuclear holocaust.
Ron Taylor, New York Mets pitcher, 1969

Joe Schultz would have been a better manager if he understood more. Of course, if he understood more, he might not have been a manager.
Jim Bouton, Seattle Pilots pitcher, on his manager, 1969

I don't walk the streets.
**Bruce Kison, Pittsburgh Pirates pitcher,
when asked if he was recognized on the streets, 1971**

My uncle dumped me in the ocean when I was six. I think I walked back underneath the water. I know I didn't walk on top.

Rocky Bridges, Triple-A Hawaii Islanders manager,
on how he learned to swim, 1972

Rocky Bridges chews tobacco because the chewing-gum industry wants no part of him. **Don Rickles, comic**

Every time I fail to smoke a cigarette between innings the opposition will score.

Earl Weaver, Baltimore Orioles manager, 1972

Looking and acting like a big-leaguer is very important to baseball people. If Jerry Rubin could hit .400, he'd still have trouble making the cut.

Jim Bouton, *I Managed Good,*
***But Boy Did They Play Bad*, 1973**

That ball has a hit in it, so I want it to get back in the ball bag and goof around with the other balls in there. Maybe it'll learn some sense and come out as a pop-up next time.

Mark Fidrych, Detroit Tigers pitcher, 1976

There ain't a left-hander in the world that can run a straight line. It's the gravitational pull on the axis of the earth that gets 'em. **Ray Miller, Baltimore Orioles coach, 1977**

Please God, let me hit one. I'll tell everybody you did it.

Reggie Jackson, New York Yankees outfielder,
pleading for a home run, 1977

Baseball players are the weirdest of all. I think it's all that organ music. **Peter Gent, *Texas Celebrity Turkey Trot*, 1978**

With ballplayers, it's either baseball or sex. It's all physical stuff. But then, we are physical animals; we try to limit our intellectual abilities because it hurts our performance.

Bill Lee, Montreal Expos pitcher, 1979

In baseball, you're supposed to sit on your ass, spit tobacco, and nod at stupid things.   **Bill Lee, 1979**

There are three types of baseball players—those who make it happen, those who watch it happen and those who wonder what happens.
Tom Lasorda, Los Angeles Dodgers manager, 1979

It was said that the first book Mickey Mantle ever finished reading was his own autobiography.
Joseph McBride, *High and Inside*, 1980

Charley Finley gave me Catfish Hunter's old jersey. By the time I got it all the wins had been used up.
Matt Keough, Oakland A's pitcher, 1981

The reason the Irish are fighting each other is that they have no other worthy opponents.
Tug McGraw, Philadelphia Phillies pitcher, 1981

Bill Lee. Another USC man. When they come out of USC, they go directly to the moon.
Lon Simmons, San Francisco Giants announcer, 1981

There is no homework.
Dan Quisenberry, Kansas City Royals pitcher,
on the best thing about baseball, 1981

You give 100 percent in the first half of the game, and if that isn't enough, in the second half you give what's left.
Yogi Berra, New York Yankees coach, 1982

He must have made that before he died.
Yogi Berra, on a Steve McQueen movie, 1982

The American League has more smut magazines in the clubhouses.
Bob Uecker, Milwaukee Brewers announcer,
on the difference between the two leagues, 1982

We had catfish today in the restaurant, and Wayne Hagen said he wouldn't eat anything that was named after a pitcher.

Lon Simmons, now an Oakland A's announcer,
on his colleague in the booth, 1982

Chapter 6

Catching

My catcher showed up and he must have been Old Man Moses. He was so old he didn't have to crouch.

Satchel Paige, Negro-leagues pitcher, 1928

I can't remember your name. But I know we used to pitch you high and outside.

Bill Dickey, New York Yankees catcher, when asked by Joe Gantenbein if he remembered him, 1943

Gimme the goddamn ball and get the hell out of here!

Vic Raschi, New York Yankees pitcher, to Yogi Berra, in a tense moment of the 1949 World Series

The infield is like a steel net held in the hand of the catcher. He is the psychologist and historian for the staff—or else his signals will give the opposition hits.

Jacques Barzun, *God's Country and Mine*, 1954

Newk, you better do somethin', because when I signal for the express you throws me the local.

> **Roy Campanella, Brooklyn Dodgers catcher,**
> **to pitcher Don Newcombe**

I didn't raise my son to be a catcher.

> **Mrs. Marciano, on why her boxer son, Rocky,**
> **didn't sign a contract with the Chicago Cubs**

I don't mind catching your fastball at all. Naturally, I'd want to have a glove on in case you might be having an especially good day.

> **Gene Green, St. Louis Cardinals catcher,**
> **to pitcher Jim Brosnan, 1959**

You gotta have a catcher. If you don't have a catcher, you'll have all passed balls.

> **Casey Stengel, New York Mets manager, on why**
> **he drafted Hobie Landrith first in the expansion draft, 1961**

I got one that can throw but can't catch, and one that can catch but can't throw, and one who can hit but can't do either.

> **Casey Stengel, New York Mets manager,**
> **on his three catchers, 1962**

When I started to throw the ball back to the pitcher harder than he was throwing to me, we changed positions.

> **Bert Blyleven, Minnesota Twins pitcher**
> **and former catcher**

I remember one time going out to the mound to talk with Bob Gibson. He told me to get back behind the batter, that the only thing I knew about pitching was it was hard to hit.

> **Tim McCarver, St. Louis Cardinals catcher, 1972**

The way to catch a knuckleball is to wait until the ball stops rolling and then pick it up.   **Bob Uecker, former catcher, 1975**

The catcher is the physical and emotional focus of every baseball game; he faces outward, surveying and guiding it all, and everyone else on the team looks in at him. The rock-hard catcher is the jewel of the movement.

Roger Angell, *Late Innings*, 1982

Chapter 7

Cities and Teams

Atlanta

Our idea of a good promotion is to get the team home from the park safely.

Bob Hope, Braves promotions director, 1977

The Atlanta Braves are in last place, where they have been for the last four years. I wonder if they signed a lease?

Hank Greenwald, San Francisco Giants announcer, 1979

I look upon baseball as a kind of little extra burden that I have. Some people have to live with diabetes, I have to live with a lousy baseball team. **Ted Turner, Braves owner, 1980**

We have no crazies or flakes or drug addicts.

**Ted Turner, on the reason for
the team's success, 1982**

Baltimore

We got no business scheduling these guys. This Baltimore out-
fit can sure fluff up your ERA.

Fred Talbot, Seattle Pilots pitcher, as he lost, 15–3, 1969

We're so bad right now that for us back-to-back home runs
means one today and another one tomorrow.

Earl Weaver, Orioles manager, 1972

Boston

The crowd was making more noise than any Boston crowd had
since the Colonials took two from the British at Concord and
Lexington.

**Robert W. Creamer,
on the 1918 World Series, in *Babe*, 1974**

Boston has two seasons: August and winter.

Billy Herman, Red Sox manager, 1965

Fenway Park, in Boston, is a lyric little bandbox of a ball park.
Everything is painted green and seems in curiously sharp
focus, like the inside of an old-fashioned peeping-type Easter
egg. **John Updike, novelist**

Twenty-five men came to the park, played a ballgame, and
took twenty-five cabs home.

Ron Luciano, umpire, on the late 1970s Red Sox

Baseball isn't a life-and-death matter, but the Red Sox are.

Mike Barnicle, *Boston Globe*, 1977

All literary men are Red Sox fans. To be a Yankee fan in
literary society is to endanger your life.

John Cheever, novelist, 1978

In Boston we believe . . . the world will break your heart some day, and we are luckier than most—we get ours broken every year, at Fenway Park. **Mordecai Richler, "Expansion," 1979**

When I'm through, I'll end up face down in the Charles River.
Bill Lee, Red Sox pitcher,
on Boston fans' dislike of him, 1979

The Red Sox are a religion. Every year we re-enact the agony and the temptation in the Garden. Baseball child's play? Hell, up here in Boston it's a passion play.
George V. Higgins, *Time*, 1980

No lefties, no speed, what's a bunt?
Bill James, sportswriter, on the Red Sox, 1981

The Yankees belong to George Steinbrenner and the Dodgers belong to Manifest Destiny, but the Red Sox, more than any other team, belong to the fans.
Steve Wulf, *Sports Illustrated*, 1981

An almost inexorable baseball law: A Red Sox ship with a single leak will always find a way to sink. . . . No team is worshipped with such a perverse sense of fatality.
Thomas Boswell,
***How Life Imitates the World Series*, 1982**

Brooklyn

Brooklyn! Is Brooklyn still in the league?
Bill Terry, New York Giants infielder,
infuriating Dodgers fans in spring 1925

Their nickname of "Bums" was at this time very appropriate. It could have referred to any checks the organization cashed.
Fresco Thompson, Dodgers executive,
on the late-1930s Dodgers

Overconfidence may cost the Dodgers sixth place.

> Edward T. Murphy, sportswriter,
> on another poor Dodgers team in the 1930s

Wait Till Next Year.

> *Brooklyn Eagle* headline, 1941,
> as Dodgers lost to the Yankees in the World Series;
> later adopted as a slogan of Dodgers fans

Dissension? We got no dissension. What we ain't got is pitchers.   Roy Campanella, Dodgers catcher, 1950

Wait till last year.

> Roger Kahn, sportswriter,
> after the Dodgers won the 1955 World Series, 1956

This is the obit on the Brooklyn Dodgers. Preliminary diagnosis indicates that the cause of death was an acute case of greed, followed by severe political complications.

> Dick Young, on the Dodgers move to Los Angeles,
> New York *Daily News*, 1957

The team was awesomely good and yet defeated. Their skills lifted everyman's spirit and their defeat joined them with everyman's existence.   Roger Kahn, *The Boys of Summer*, 1973

They brought me up to the Brooklyn Dodgers, which at that time was in Brooklyn.

> Casey Stengel, New York Mets manager, 1962

For the next twenty years, I believed that the three worst people of the twentieth century were Hitler, Stalin and Walter O'Malley. I never forgave any of them.

> Pete Hamill, on the Dodgers' move,
> New York *Daily News*, 1981

Short of having your mother or father die, losing the Dodgers was the heaviest thing that could have happened.

> David Ritz, *Sport*, 1981

Chicago

I'd rather be a lamppost in Chicago than a millionaire in any other city.

William A. Hulbert,
Chicago White Stockings president, 1875

New York didn't need that 1969 pennant . . . all Cub fans wanted was that one measly pennant. It would have kept us happy until the twenty-first century. But New York took that from us and I can never forgive that.

Mike Royko, *Chicago Sun-Times*, 1981

The Chicago Cubs are like Rush Street—a lot of singles, but no action.   **Joe Garagiola, broadcaster, on the 1970s Cubs**

One thing about the Chicago Bears. When the season starts, it sure takes the heat off us Cubs.

Bill Madlock, Cubs infielder, 1975

Things were so bad in Chicago last summer that by the fifth inning we were selling hot dogs to go.

Ken Brett, White Sox pitcher, 1975

Being a White Sox fan meant measuring victory in terms of defeat. A 6–5 defeat was a good day. A big rally was Wally Moses doubling down the right-field line.

Jean Shepherd, Chicago humorist, 1975

There is no off-season in Chicago. It is only when the teams start playing that the fans lose interest.

Steve Daley, *Chicago Tribune* columnist, c.1975

When you play with the Cubs, it's like playing with heavy shoes on. I had to be de-Cubbed.

Pete LaCock, former Cubs first baseman, 1976

You have to have a certain dullness of mind and spirit to play here. I went through psychoanalysis, and that helped me deal with my Cubness.   **Jim Brosnan, former Cubs pitcher, 1981**

Other teams won and made it look easy. The Cubs lost and made it look hard.
        David Brinkley, "NBC Magazine," NBC-TV, 1981

This is going to be a funny monologue tonight. Look, if the Cubs can win a game anything can happen.
        Johnny Carson, "The Tonight Show," NBC-TV, 1981

When we were kids, we used to go to the circus all the time—only we called it Wrigley Field.   Tom Dreesen, comic, 1981

You have fourteen guys who can't play Triple-A, the free-agent pickings are slim and there's nothing in the minors. Good luck.
        Jimmy Piersall, former White Sox announcer,
        to new Cubs general manager Dallas Green, 1981

Since 1946, the Cubs have had two problems: They put too few runs on the scoreboard and the other guys put too many. So what is the new management improving? The scoreboard.
        George Will, *Washington Post*, 1982

At Yankee Stadium the fans throw bottles from the outfield. At Comiskey Park, they throw them from the box seats.
        Eddie Einhorn, White Sox owner, 1982

I heard how these new players, these "gamers," were going to cure everything. Instead of curing the disease, they caught it.
        Herman Franks, former Cubs manager,
        on the new Cubs, 1982

Cincinnati

Cincy is a dry town—as dry as the Atlantic Ocean.
        Damon Runyon,
        writing on the eve of the World Series, 1919

It's possible to spend money anywhere in the world if you put your mind to it, something I proved conclusively by running up huge debts in Cincinnati.

Leo Durocher, Cincinnati Reds shortstop, 1933

Ted Kluszewski was on third. Somebody like Odrowski on second, maybe Timowitz on first. Boy, was I sweatin', hopin' nobody'd get a hit and I wouldn't have to call all them names.

Dizzy Dean, broadcaster

In Cincinnati after two o'clock, the only people you see are bartenders, ballplayers, and cab drivers.

Jim Brosnan, *Pennant Race*, 1962

It's a good thing I stayed in Cincinnati for four years—it took me that long to learn how to spell it.

Rocky Bridges, former infielder, 1972

Sometimes I think they've intentionally maintained a mediocre pitching staff to let the opposing hitters make contact and provide their fielders with a chance to show off their skills.

Marty Bell, sportswriter, on the 1970s Reds, 1978

You give us the pitching some of these clubs have and no one could touch us. But God has a way of not arranging that, because it isn't as much fun.

**Sparky Anderson,
manager of the "Big Red Machine," 1978**

Cleveland

Maybe they ought to change our name to the Cleveland Utility Company. We don't have anything but utility men.

Lou Camilli, Indians infielder, 1971

The only good thing about playing in Cleveland is you don't have to make road trips there.

Richie Scheinblum, former Indians outfielder, 1973

In twenty-five years, the two most exciting moments have been Tito Francona's TV commercials for Central National Bank and Valmy Thomas' groin injury.

Bennett Tramer, *Inside Sports*, 1979

The A's leave after this game for Cleveland. It was only by a 13–12 vote that they decided to go.

Lon Simmons, Oakland A's announcer, 1982

I always liked working Indian games, because they were usually out of the pennant race by the end of April and there was never too much pressure on the umpires.

Ron Luciano, *The Umpire Strikes Back*, 1982

Detroit

Club officials apparently believe that I can live for a year on the fruit and vegetables which thoughtful Detroit fans contributed during the last game of the World Series.

**Ducky Medwick,
St. Louis Cardinals outfielder, holding out, 1935**

We are constitutionally opposed to the creation of young sports millionaries. **John Fetzer, Tigers owner, 1978**

Billy Martin sent me up for Al Kaline once. I made an out. I told him, "Keep doing this and you're going to get both of us run out of town." **Gates Brown, former Tigers outfielder, 1982**

Houston

Some of the bugs there are twin-engine jobs.

Sandy Koufax, Los Angeles Dodgers pitcher, 1961

This is the only town where women wear insect repellant instead of perfume.

Richie Ashburn, New York Mets outfielder, 1962

It isn't much, but we call it home.
> Jim Owens, Astros pitcher, on the Astrodome, 1964

They don't bother us none. We're still working on grounders.
> Casey Stengel, New York Mets manager, asked
> if his team would practice fly balls in the Astrodome, 1965

Our fans are more like the ones they have out in California. We don't have any of those rowdies or semi-delinquents who follow the Mets. **Judge Roy Hofheinz, Astros owner, 1966**

Texas has a rather confusing image. It's the country of rugged outdoors people, where they play baseball and football under a roof. **Bill Vaughn, *Half the Battle*, 1967**

The Houston Astrodome is the biggest hairdryer in the world.
> Joe Pepitone, Astros infielder, 1970

No one booed an Astro player. No one got into a fight; a fight at the Astrodome would be as shocking as fisticuffs in the College of Cardinals. **Roger Angell, *The Summer Game*, 1972**

Just think, if Houston and Montreal stay on top, it will be the first time the National League playoffs will take place entirely outside the United States.
> Hank Greenwald, San Francisco Giants announcer, 1979

I like the lifestyle in Houston. You can wear your jeans here without people thinking you're trying to be stylish.
> Don Sutton, Astros pitcher, 1980

They're just a nice bunch of guys. The Astros not only help you up after you've stolen on them, but they dust you off.
> Phil Garner, Astros infielder,
> asking his teammates to get tough, 1982

Kansas City

Kansas City wasn't the fun spot in my day that it is now.
> Casey Stengel, New York Yankees manager, 1955

I wasn't going to no goddamn Kansas City. They got a lot of stews there, but what the hell do you do with them after you ball them—there's no place to go.

Bo Belinsky, former pitcher, 1972

The way we have been playing I might tell my players not to cross the picket lines.

**Whitey Herzog, Royals manager,
on the umpires' strike, 1979**

Los Angeles

They had room at the Los Angeles Coliseum for 93,000 people and two outfielders. **Lindsey Nelson, sportscaster**

The girls all look like Brigitte Bardot. Come to think of it, some of the men do, too.

Jim Murray, *The Best of Jim Murray*, 1965

Things have been a little tough. Do you think you could get the President to give federal aid to the team—as a disaster area?

**Johnny Carson,
to Lillian Carter, "The Tonight Show," NBC-TV, 1977**

They get some 747 moths here in Los Angeles. They take the coat *home* and eat it.

Lon Simmons, San Francisco Giants announcer, 1978

Say "Dodgers" and people know you're talking about baseball. Say "Braves" and they ask, "What reservation?" Say "Reds" and they think of communism. Say "Padres" and they look around for a priest. **Tom Lasorda, Dodgers manager, 1979**

Only in Los Angeles do the guys in the radio booth wear make-up. **Gary Park, San Francisco sportscaster, 1981**

Maybe this has been the trouble with our team this year. The players have been trying to do two jobs—trying to run the club and play ball at the same time.

Buzzie Bavasi, California Angels vice-president, 1981

If the Southern California teams keep beating up on us we're not going to give you any more of our water.

Lon Simmons, Oakland A's announcer, 1982

Milwaukee

We didn't want to weaken the rest of the league.

Frank Lane, Brewers general manager,
on why he didn't make any trades in the off-season, 1972

Minnesota

I think this is great. The ball really shoots out of here. Now if we can only learn to hit it.

Calvin Griffith, Twins owner, on the new Metrodome, 1982

Calvin Griffith returned from the fishing season opener with his limit of walleyes. Calvin immediately took the walleyes to a grocery store and traded them for a package of Mrs. Paul's frozen fish sticks and ten dollars in cash.

Charley Walters, on the quality of Griffith's trades,
St. Paul Pioneer Press, **1982**

Montreal

One of our starters would have to drop dead and they are all younger than I am.

Bill Lee, Expos pitcher,
trying to break into the lineup, 1981

New York

It's great to be young and a Giant.

Larry Doyle, Giants infielder

This isn't just a ball club! This is Murderers Row!

Arthur Robinson, New York sportswriter,
on the Yankees, 1927

It's always the same. Combs walks. Koenig singles. Ruth hits one out of the park. Gehrig doubles. Lazzeri triples. Then Dugan goes in the dirt on his can.

Joe Dugan, Yankees infielder, 1927

They don't just beat you. They break your heart.

Joe Judge, Washington Senators infielder,
on the Yankees, 1927

Shut up you guys or I'll put on a Yankee uniform and scare the shit out of you.

Waite Hoyt, Pittsburgh Pirates pitcher,
to opposing players razzing him, 1933

Rooting for the Yankees is like rooting for U.S. Steel.

Joe E. Lewis, comic

It may be noted that the Yankees are the least popular of all baseball clubs, because they win, which leaves nothing to "if" about. **A. J. Liebling, journalist**

Yes, and so is everyone else in the league.

Groucho Marx, upon hearing
that Leo Durocher was leading the Giants, 1951

Branca throws. There's a long fly. . . . It's gonna be . . . I believe . . . The Giants win the pennant! The Giants win the pennant! The Giants win the pennant! The Giants win the pennant! . . . I don't believe it. I don't believe it. I will *not* believe it.

Russ Hodges, Giants announcer,
broadcasting the Giants/Dodgers playoff game, 1951

I'd like to thank the good Lord for making me a Yankee.

Joe DiMaggio, Yankees outfielder

I feel bad about the kids, but I haven't seen many of their fathers lately.

Horace Stoneham, Giants owner, asked how he felt about moving the Giants to San Francisco, 1957

The Mets is a very good thing. They give everybody a job. Just like the WPA [Works Project Association].

Billy Loes, former pitcher, 1962

They've shown me ways to lose I never knew existed.

Casey Stengel, Mets manager, 1962

I have a son, and I make him watch the Mets. I want him to know life. It's a history lesson. He'll understand the Depression when they teach it to him in school.

Toots Shor, New York restaurateur, 1962

People are always saying that one-eighth of an inch is the difference between winning and losing baseball. With the Mets, it is three inches.   **Murray Kempton, *Sport*, 1962**

If I have to be a benchwarmer for the New York Mets I'll commit suicide.

Richie Ashburn, Mets outfielder, retiring from the game, 1963

If everybody on this team commenced breaking up the furniture every time we did bad, there'd be no place to sit.

Casey Stengel, Mets manager, after Ron Swoboda tore up the dugout, 1963

Just when my fellows learn to hit in this ball park, they're gonna tear it down.

Casey Stengel, Mets manager, on the Polo Grounds, 1965

I just found out what's driving me crazy—it's baseball.

Ron Taylor, Mets pitcher

If the Mets can win the World Series, the United States can get out of Viet Nam.   **Tom Seaver, Mets pitcher, 1969**

The last miracle that I did was the 1969 Mets.

**George Burns,
portraying God in the film, *Oh, God!*, screenplay by Larry
Gelbart, based on the novel by Avery Corman, 1977**

Fifteen minutes after the Mets had clinched their championship, their followers had torn up the Shea Stadium surface. . . . And, being true Mets fans with their roots in 1962, they missed first base.   **Leonard Koppett, *The New York Mets*, 1970**

If I was playing in New York, they'd name a candy bar after me.   **Reggie Jackson, Oakland A's outfielder, 1973**

Never sell the Yankees short. They played great the last three months. They'll never play that well again as long as they have assholes.

**Johnny Pesky, Boston Red Sox coach, as the
Yankees went 52–22 to win the pennant, 1978**

We're spending all our money to try to solve the problems in the Middle East. We ought to be spending it on educating these idiots here.

**Reggie Smith, Los Angeles Dodgers outfielder,
on Yankees fans at the World Series, 1978**

I could never play in New York. The first time I ever came into a game there, I got in the bullpen car and they told me to lock the doors.

Mike Flanagan, Baltimore Orioles pitcher, 1979

The more self-centered and egotistical a guy is, the better ballplayer he's going to be. You take a team with twenty-five assholes and I'll show you a pennant. I'll show you the New York Yankees.   **Bill Lee, Montreal Expos pitcher, 1979**

When I was a kid, I wanted to play baseball and join the circus. With the Yankees, I've been able to do both.

Graig Nettles, Yankees infielder, 1980

Hating the Yankees is as American as pizza pie, unwed mothers and cheating on your income tax.
Mike Royko, *Chicago Sun-Times*, 1981

It's a fickle town, a tough town. They getcha, boy. They don't let you escape with minor scratches and bruises. They put scars on you here.
Reggie Jackson, New York Yankees outfielder, 1981

The Yankees are pretty strong but they are weak on the disabled list. That's why they picked up Bruce Hobson, so they can put him on the disabled list.
Hank Greenwald, San Francisco Giants announcer, 1982

We have deep depth.   **Yogi Berra, Yankees coach, 1982**

Reggie Jackson, Thurman Munson and George Steinbrenner: Every once in a while one of them would lie and say he liked the other two.   **Dick Schaap, "PBS Latenight," PBS-TV, 1982**

Oakland

If everything the press says about us playing best when we're mad is true, then we've got this thing wrapped up.
Sal Bando, A's infielder, on dissension, 1973

This fucking city can't do anything right.
Charlie Finley, A's owner, after there was a small civic turnout for his championship team, 1974

It makes you rethink the importance of being in the major leagues.   **Jim Marshall, A's manager, on his 54–108 team, 1979**

Our biggest problem is lack of talent.
Dave Revering, A's infielder, 1979

A time or two before there might have been a fair-sized crowd here, but if there were 30,000 of them, only 3,000 were rooting for us.   **Steve McCatty, A's pitcher, 1981**

Billy Martin would ask somebody on the bench what pitch was just thrown, to see if you're paying attention. I can remember in 1979 when you'd have trouble finding out from our bench who was up, what town we were in and what day it was!

Matt Keough, A's pitcher, 1981

Philadelphia

We had three teams: one playing that afternoon, one coming in that night, and one leaving the next morning.

**Jimmy Dykes, Athletics infielder,
on the high turnover, early 1900s**

If they think I'd stand there in that sun and pitch another nine innings waiting for our bums to make another run, they're crazy.

**Jack Nabors, Athletics pitcher, wild-pitching in the
winning run after the score was tied 1–1 in the ninth, 1916**

On a clear day they could see seventh place.

**Fresco Thompson, Los Angeles Dodgers executive,
on the late-1920s Phillies**

If the Giants win but two of four/And the Dodgers six of ten/The Phillies, as in days of yore/Will finish last again.

George Phair, *New York American*, c.1920s

Don't bet on the A's.

**Connie Mack, Athletics owner,
when asked for a tip by a cabdriver, 1940**

That's too bad; they're the only team I can beat.

Dave Cole, pitcher, on being sold to the Phillies, 1955

Philadelphia fans would boo funerals, an Easter egg hunt, a parade of armless war vets, and the Liberty Bell.

Bo Belinsky, former Phillies pitcher, 1972

If I can get the Philadelphia Phillies to win the World Series after a hundred years, then I can do anything.
                    Pete Rose, Phillies infielder, 1979

Pittsburgh

Pittsburgh is such a tough town even the canaries sing bass there. **Arthur "Bugs" Baer, sportswriter**

The trouble with these guys is that after you've been with them a couple of weeks you start to play like them.
                    Sid Gordon, Pirates outfielder, 1951

You guys have a fifty-fifty team. You get 'em out in the club-house but lose in the field.
                    Rogers Hornsby, Cincinnati Reds manager, 1952

Dorothy Lamour: You still have Pirates in America?
Bing Crosby: Yeah. But there's nothing to worry about, they're probably hiding in the cellar someplace.
                    ***Road To Bali*, screenplay by Frank Butler,**
                    Hal Kanter, and William Morrow, 1952

One club will watch your delivery and say, "Oh, boy, here comes a fastball," and they'll jump on it. Others say, "Oh, boy, here's a changeup." The Pirates just say, "Oh, boy, here comes a baseball." **Don Sutton, Los Angeles Dodgers pitcher, 1973**

If San Salvador falls, that could mean the rest of the Spanish-speaking world will follow: Tijuana, Miami, not to mention the Pittsburgh Pirates.
                    Melanie Chartoff, "Fridays," ABC-TV, 1981

St. Louis

First in shoes, first in booze, and last in the American League.
                    Browns' slogan, late 1930s

We could finish first or in an asylum.

Frankie Frisch,
manager of the Cardinals Gashouse Gang, 1936

On that club you had to make your own excitement.

Joe Garagiola, catcher, on the 1949 Cardinals

The Mets achieved total incompetence in a single year, while the Browns worked industriously for almost a decade to gain equal proficiency. **Bill Veeck,** *Veeck as in Wreck,* **1962**

So many guys come and go here that if we won the pennant, our shares would be $50 apiece.

Danny Cater, Cardinals infielder, 1975

We need three kinds of pitching: left-handed, right-handed and relief. **Whitey Herzog, Cardinals manager, 1980**

The Giants played a game here last year, and they said the temperature on the field was 143 degrees. With the wind chill factor it was 140.

Hank Greenwald, San Francisco Giants announcer, 1980

There are so many new faces around here, I thought I'd been traded.

Ken Oberkfell, Cardinals infielder, at spring training, 1981

San Diego

The good news is that we may stay in San Diego. The bad news, I guess, is the same thing.

Buzzie Bavasi, Padres president,
not happy with attendance, 1976

The club is a helluva lot of fun, like my wife, but there's no profit in either one. **Ray Kroc, Padres owner, 1978**

I have nothing against the city, but it's a little enclave, a corner of the country. What starts in San Diego stays there.

Dave Winfield, former Padres outfielder, 1981

Every season it's predicted that the Padres are about to go somewhere. And every year it turns out to be the beach.

Thomas Boswell, *Inside Sports*, 1981

We've got a whole bunch of new players. But I don't think they're the right ones. **Ozzie Smith, Padres shortstop, 1981**

Tradition here [St. Louis] is Stan Musial coming into the clubhouse and making the rounds. Tradition in San Diego is Nate Colbert coming into the clubhouse and trying to sell you a used car. **Bob Shirley, former Padres pitcher, 1981**

San Francisco

The closer you get to these guys, the worse they look.

Tom Sheehan, Giants manager, 1960

The Giants were supposed to have a new motto: "Shut up and deal." **Alvin Dark, Giants manager, 1961**

Candlestick Park was built on the water. It should have been built under it.

Roger Maris, New York Yankees outfielder, 1961

What a town. They boo Willie Mays and cheer Khrushchev.

Frank Coniff, New York writer, 1962

A business executive is standing in his office looking down over the city. . . . Suddenly, a falling figure shoots past the window. "Oh, oh," the man says, glancing at his chronometer. "It must be June. There go the Giants."

Jim Murray, *The Best of Jim Murray*, 1965

If they check the upper deck, they might find Patty Hearst hiding out.

Bobby Murcer, Giants outfielder, on the small crowds, 1975

Candlestick Park. That's the ninth blunder of the world.

Herb Caen, *San Francisco Chronicle*, 1980

There's a good crowd tonight. I was going to say people are strung out all over the place, but people might take that literally. **Hank Greenwald, Giants announcer, 1981**

What they should do is give Candlestick Park back to the city and use it as a prison. Then, they could sentence the convicts to playing baseball . . . naked.

Jim Lefebvre, Giants coach, 1981

Whenever the Giants call to talk about trades, I bet more than one general manager has had to hold a pillow over his face to keep from laughing into the phone.

Lowell Cohn, *San Francisco Chronicle*, 1982

Seattle

We already knew we were going to lose the second game, too. We just didn't know what the score was going to be.

Jim Bouton, Pilots pitcher, 1969

If we get a lead tonight, boys, let's call time out.

Fred Talbot, Pilots pitcher, 1969

The Seattle Mariners tried a novel promotional gimmick Saturday night—winning. **E. M. Swift, *Sports Illustrated*, 1981**

The only thing we led baseball in was team meetings.

Richie Zisk, Mariners infielder, 1981

Being named manager of the Seattle Mariners is like becoming head chef at McDonalds.

Charles Bricker, *San Jose Mercury*, 1981

Toronto

If this had been a prison break, there would have been twenty-four guys behind me.

Rick Bosetti, Blue Jays outfielder, upon being traded, 1981

Washington

Washington—first in war, first in peace, last in the American League. **Charles Dryden, writer, on the Senators, early 1900s**

When the Yankees hit the ball it turned into a jackrabbit, while every time the Senators touched it up it proved to be nothing but the good old-fashioned beanbag.
Paul Gallico, sportswriter, on the "live ball," 1927

What we're trying to do here is make chicken salad out of chicken shit. **Joe Kuhel, Senators manager, 1949**

For the Washington Senators, the worst time of the year is the baseball season. **Roger Kahn, sportswriter, 1960s**

We cheer for the Senators, we pray for the Senators, and we hope that the Supreme Court doesn't declare that unconstitutional. **Lyndon B. Johnson, vice president, 1962**

There is a federal law which forbids them to win.
John Steinbeck, novelist, 1965

The Washington players need years of coaching, not days. The Washington boys need to be reborn—not remade.
Ted Williams, Senators manager, 1969

Chapter 8

Coaches and Scouts

This boy is wild low. He doesn't have enough stuff to be wild high.

**Fresco Thompson, Brooklyn Dodgers scout,
report to general manager Branch Rickey**

All coaches religiously carry fungo bats in the spring to ward off suggestions that they are not working.

Jim Brosnan, *The Long Season*, 1960

You think *you've* got it bad. I've got to room with a *coach.*

Jim Owens, Houston Astros pitcher, 1967

It's a boring job. But people who become coaches are not easily bored. You ever see a baby play with a rattle for two hours?   **Jim Bouton, *Ball Four*, 1970**

Coaches are an integral part of any manager's team. Especially if they're good pinochle players.   **Earl Weaver, *Winning!*, 1972**

Whoever answers the bullpen phone.
**Chuck Estrada, Texas Rangers coach,
on who he brings in for relief on his last-place team, 1973**

They're persistent people; I heard about one scout who, to sign a prospect, got engaged to his spinster sister; they say she would have scared a hog.
Gaylord Perry, *Me and the Spitter*, 1972

You feel guilty telling the batters to go out there and get a hit. They look at you funny, as if to say, "You try it."
Ray Miller, Baltimore Orioles coach, 1980

You've got a lot of cute stuff. But son, there's only one thing we're looking for, and that's a pitcher who can tear the catcher's head off with a fastball. You get one of those, come on back.
**Tom Wolfe, writer, quoting a scout
at his tryout with the New York Giants, 1981**

Don't feel bad, I walked a guy once.
Art Fowler, Oakland A's coach, advising his pitcher, 1981

Chapter 9

Drinking and Debauchery

It depends on the length of the game.
> **King Kelly, Chicago White Stockings outfielder,
> asked if he drinks while playing, c.1890s**

Whenever a ball looks like this:

⊖
⊖
⊖

Take a chance on the middle one.
> *Cincinnati Enquirer*, **advice to drunken hitters, 1903**

There is much less drinking now than there was before 1927, because I quit drinking on May 24, 1927.
> **Rabbit Maranville, Boston Braves infielder, 1928**

I called myself a semipro although it might have been closer to three eighths. Too much beer in Bustleton is what stopped me. **Arthur "Bugs" Baer, *Collier's*, 1942**

I am quite sure the statistics will show that the greatest number of successes have been scored by those who led moderately dirty lives.

W. O. McGeehan, sportswriter, writing about Babe Ruth

I think beer drinkers win more games than those chocolate-soda drinkers.

Frank Lane, Kansas City Athletics general manager, 1961

Ten-thirty? I'm not even done throwing up at that hour.

**Jim Pagliaroni, Seattle Pilots catcher,
when told to take batting practice at an early hour, 1969**

If you're trying to outdrink San Francisco, you're overmatched.

**Casey Stengel, New York Yankees manager,
to Mickey Mantle and Whitey Ford,
in town for the World Series, 1962**

Hell, if I didn't drink or smoke, I'd win twenty games every year. It's easy if you don't drink or smoke or horse around.

Whitey Ford, New York Yankees pitcher, 1965

It shows what you can accomplish if you stay up all night drinking whiskey all the time.

**Toots Shor, restaurateur, on the Hall of Fame induction
of Whitey Ford and Mickey Mantle, 1974**

Ninety percent I'll spend on good times, women and Irish whiskey. The other ten percent I'll probably waste.

**Tug McGraw, Philadelphia Phillies pitcher,
on his salary increase, 1975**

If I were a Tibetan priest and ate everything perfect, maybe I'd live to be 105. The way I'm going now, I'll probably only make it to 102. I'll give away 3 years to beer.

Bill Lee, Montreal Expos pitcher, 1979

I never took the game home with me. I always left it in some bar. **Bob Lemon, former manager, 1976**

The chief duty of team captains was to try to keep at least some of the players sober.
>
> **Glenn Dickey, on the early days of the league,**
> ***The History of National League Baseball*, 1979**

I made a vow in church when I was a kid that I would not drink until I was eighteen. I've made up for it since.
>
> **Billy Martin, Oakland A's manager, 1980**

When Billy Martin reaches for a bar tab, his arm shrinks six inches. **Tom Lasorda, Los Angeles Dodgers manager, 1981**

The last time the Bees were in Reno, I lost the bus and two outfielders, but I won a shortstop and a bat.
>
> **Rocky Bridges, manager, Triple-A San Jose Bees, 1972**

True grit: trying to make it through a hangover without a greenie.
>
> **Jim Pagliaroni, Seattle Pilots catcher,**
> **on amphetamines, 1969**

Boys, if you get caught with Mary Jane, you better be hitting four-fucking-eighty at the All-Star break.
>
> **A coach, on marijuana, c.1970s**

Amphetamines improved my performance about five percent. Unfortunately, in my particular case that wasn't enough.
>
> **Jim Bouton, New York Yankees pitcher, 1971**

Any girl who doesn't want to fuck can leave now.
>
> **Babe Ruth, New York Yankees outfielder,**
> **at a party in Detroit, 1928**

Being with a woman all night never hurt no professional baseball player. It's staying up all night looking for a woman that does him in. **Casey Stengel, New York Yankees manager**

You gotta learn that if you don't get it by midnight, chances are you ain't gonna get it, and if you do, it ain't worth it.
>
> **Casey Stengel, to players late for curfew**

With women you don't have to talk your head off. You just say a word and let them fill in from there. What they fill in can be mighty interesting.

Satchel Paige, *Maybe I'll Pitch Forever*, 1962

To keep yourself from being ruined, every time you think you want some sex, jack off, and then take a dollar and put it in the trunk of your car and forget about it. You'll keep your fastball, and you'll have a lot of money at the end of the season. **Rube Haggerty, pitching coach, to rookies**

If you need a workout go down to a whorehouse.

Joe Schultz, Seattle Pilots manager, to a pitcher who said he needed more work, 1969

Boys, I had all the ingredients for a great piece of ass last night—plenty of time, and a hard-on. All I lacked was a broad.

Ray Oyler, Seattle Pilots infielder, 1969

We prefer *wham, bam,* thank-you-ma'am affairs. In fact, if we're spotted taking a girl out to dinner we're accused of "wining and dining," which is bad form.

Jim Bouton, *Ball Four*, 1970

Don't come, kid, you're pitching tonight.

Jim Bouton, quoting an older pitcher to a kid at a gang bang, 1971

The reader may wonder how in the world the girls know where to find the players. So do I. They know more about us than our front offices do. **Curt Flood, *The Way It Is*, 1971**

Say you pick her up at seven o'clock. Well, then grab her where it tickles at 7:05. No go? Tough, but hell it's early yet. There's still time to call another broad. You'd be surprised. Some damned famous broads say okay quick.

Leo Durocher, Houston Astros manager, 1972

I only go out with girls when I'm horny.

Mark Fidrych, Detroit Tigers pitcher, 1976

The trouble with bed checks is you usually disturb your best players. **Dick Siebert, minor-league coach, 1977**

People who are in love never want to hurt anybody, you know that? It's only horny people who shoot people.
Ted Turner, Atlanta Braves owner, 1978

Today's players don't even womanize as much as yesterday's. They don't have to. The women manize.
Charles Einstein, *Willie's Time*, 1979

I've seldom seen a horny ballplayer walk into a bar and *not* let out exactly what he did for a living.
Johnny Bench, *Catch You Later*, 1979

Chuck Tanner used to have a bedcheck just for me every night. No problem. My bed was always there.
Jim Rooker, former pitcher, 1981

Chapter 10

Equipment

Anybody with any sense knows that bats are like ballplayers. They hate cold weather.

> **Joe Jackson, Chicago White Sox outfielder, on why he took his bats back to South Carolina at the end of the season, 1916**

A ball bat is a wondrous weapon.

> **Ty Cobb, Detroit Tigers outfielder**

When you hold the ball between your thumb and forefinger, you can hear a rabbit's pulsebeat.

> **Westbrook Pegler, New York columnist, on the 1920s "live ball"**

They fixed up a ball that if you don't miss it entirely it will clear the fence.   **Ring Lardner, on the "live ball" of the 1920s**

I add twenty points to my average if I know I look bitchin' out there.

> **Dick Stuart, Pittsburgh Pirates infielder, on his uniform**

I don't know why, but I can run faster in tight pants.
Phil Linz, Philadelphia Phillies infielder, 1966

Any baseball is beautiful. No other small package comes as close to the ideal in design and utility. It is a perfect object for a man's hand. Pick it up and it instantly suggests its purpose; it is meant to be thrown a considerable distance— thrown hard and with precision.
Roger Angell, *Five Seasons*, 1977

I'm going to retire. No way will I wear those damn hotpants.
Bobby Bonds, on being traded to the Chicago White Sox with their turn-of-the-century uniforms, 1978

The human hand is made complete by the addition of a baseball. **Paul Dickson, *The Official Explanations*, 1980**

I just figured if the resin bag is out there, you're supposed to use it.
Gaylord Perry, Atlanta Braves pitcher, on his "puffball," hurled amidst a cloud from the resin bag, 1981

I owe my success to expansion pitching, a short right-field fence and my hollow bats.
Norm Cash, former American League batting champion, 1981

No, sir, the cork is in the arms.
George Foster, Cincinnati Reds outfield, asked if he put cork in his bat, 1981

Bill Buckner had a nineteen-game hitting streak going and always wore the same underwear. Of course, he didn't have any friends. **Lenny Randle, Seattle Mariners infielder, 1981**

I love doubleheaders. That way I get to keep my uniform on longer.
Tom Lasorda, Los Angeles Dodgers manager, 1982

Chapter 11

Exercise, Diet, and Injuries

I took the two most expensive aspirins in history.
**Wally Pipp, New York Yankees infielder,
replaced because of a headache by Lou Gehrig,
who went on to play 2130 straight games, 1925**

I got a jackass back in Oklahoma, and you can work him from sunup till sundown, and he ain't never going to win the Kentucky Derby.   **Pepper Martin, St. Louis Cardinals infielder**

The worst of this is that I no longer can see my penis when I stand up.
  Babe Ruth, New York Yankees outfielder, on his large belly

Fractured, hell! The damn thing's broken.
**Dizzy Dean, St. Louis Cardinals pitcher,
when told his toe was fractured**

In Peck Memorial Hospital.
**Pete Reiser, Brooklyn Dodgers outfielder,
asked where he thought he'd finish the season, 1946**

Mr. Hornsby, tell me, are you trainin' Ol' Satch for relief pitchin' or for the army?

Satchel Paige, St. Louis Browns pitcher, to manager Rogers Hornsby, 1952

(1) Avoid fried foods which angry up the blood. (2) If your stomach disputes you, lie down and pacify it with cool thoughts. (3) Keep the juices flowing by jangling around gently as you move. (4) Go very light on the vices, such as carrying on in society. The social ramble ain't restful. (5) Avoid running at all times. (6) Don't look back. Something might be gaining on you.

Satchel Paige, "How to Stay Young," *Collier's*, 1953

If running is so important, Jesse Owens would be a twenty-game winner. **Art Fowler, Cincinnati Reds pitcher**

The only reason I don't like to run is that it makes me tired.

Art Fowler

Carrots might be good for my eyes, but they won't straighten out the curve ball. **Carl Furillo, Brooklyn Dodgers outfielder**

You mix two jiggers of Scotch to one jigger of Metrecal. So far I've lost five pounds and my driver's license.

Rocky Bridges, Cincinnati Reds infielder, on his new diet, 1956

I checked out Frank Lary's fastball on my jaw. The trouble with having a wired jaw is that you can never tell when you're sleepy—you can't yawn.

Rocky Bridges, Washington Senators infielder, 1958

The way our luck has been lately, our fellows have been getting hurt on their days off.

Casey Stengel, New York Mets manager, 1962

I've got more miles run than innings pitched, I know that.

Howie Nunn, Cincinnati Reds pitcher, 1964

Felt pretty good when I got up this morning. But I got over it.
Smokey Burgess, Chicago White Sox catcher, 1967

All that running and exercise can do for you is make you healthy. **Denny McLain, Detroit Tigers pitcher, 1971**

I've always felt a lot of pitching coaches made a living out of running pitchers so they wouldn't have to spend that same time teaching them how to pitch.
Johnny Sain, pitching coach, 1972

Fat guys need idols, too.
**Mickey Lolich, Detroit Tigers pitcher
(six feet, 230 pounds), 1972**

If I knew I was gonna live this long, I'd have taken better care of myself.
Mickey Mantle, former outfielder, age forty-six, 1978

You never know with these psychosomatic injuries. You have to take your time with them.
Jim Palmer, Baltimore Orioles pitcher, 1978

I have a grandfather who's eighty-seven years old, and he hasn't had a hard-on for the last five years. If that Dr. Cowens can manipulate Catfish Hunter's arm and bring it back to life, I'm gonna have him play with my grandfather's dick.
Lou Piniella, New York Yankees outfielder, 1978

When they operated on my arm, I asked them to put in Koufax' fastball. They did. But it turned out to be Mrs. Koufax.
**Tommy John, Los Angeles Dodgers pitcher,
on his "bionic arm" operation, 1979**

First triple I ever had.
**Lefty Gomez, former pitcher,
on his triple-bypass heart surgery, 1979**

Did you ever see a monkey with a cramp?
Bill Lee, Montreal Expos pitcher, on his banana diet, 1979

I haven't run into a bad meal yet. I postpone a few, but I never miss any.

Tom Lasorda, Los Angeles Dodgers manager, 1979

If the human body recognized agony and frustration, people would never run marathons, have babies or play baseball.

Carlton Fisk, Boston Red Sox catcher, 1979

My problem's, uh, behind me now.

George Brett, Kansas City Royals infielder,
after hemorrhoid surgery during the World Series, 1980

The X-rays came back negative? All X-rays are negative.

Lon Simmons, Oakland A's announcer, 1981

If the guys on the bench were as good as the guys you have out there, they'd be out there in the first place.

Frank Robinson, San Francisco Giants manager,
on why injuries hurt a team, 1981

Let's not overdo this. I'm an umpire, remember? I only have to call the bases, I don't have to steal them.

Eric "Rerun" Gregg, umpire, to a trainer
helping him lose some of his 300-plus pounds, 1981

I'm a light eater. When it gets light, I start eating.

Tommy John, New York Yankees pitcher, 1981

I didn't want Dr. Jobe building a swimming pool with my knee.

Steve Howe, Los Angeles Dodgers pitcher,
refusing an operation, 1982

Chapter 12

Famous Last Words

I'd be the laughingstock of baseball if I changed the best left-hander in the game into an outfielder.
    Ed Barrow, Boston Red Sox manager, on Babe Ruth, 1918

Ruth's twenty-nine homers were more spectacular than useful; they didn't help the Red Sox get out of sixth place.
    Harry Frazee, Boston Red Sox owner,
    on trading Babe Ruth to New York, 1920

Baseball is bigger than any one man. . . . Baseball is a public trust, not merely a money-making industry.
    Ford Frick, National League president

There is no chance of night baseball ever becoming popular in the bigger cities because high-class baseball cannot be played under artificial lights.
    Clark Griffith, Washington Senators owner, 1935

Pitch him low.
>> Bob Swift, Detroit Tigers catcher, advising
>> his pitcher how to pitch to midget Eddie Gaedel, 1951

Far into the night rang shouts of revelry in Flatbush. Brooklyn at long last has won a World Series and now let someone suggest moving the Dodgers elsewhere!
>> John Drebinger, *The New York Times,* 1955

The only way I can hit .300 is if there is something physically wrong with me. Pete Rose, Cincinnati Reds infielder, 1963

I hate [Billy] Martin because he plays tough. But if I played for him, I'd probably love him.
>> Reggie Jackson, Oakland A's outfielder, 1972

I won't be active in the day-to-day operations of the club at all. I can't spread myself so thin. I've got enough headaches with my shipping company.
>> George Steinbrenner, announcing his purchase
>> of the New York Yankees, 1973

My epitaph is inescapable. It will read: "He sent a midget up to bat." Bill Veeck, Chicago White Sox owner, 1976

I don't want to fight you. Little kids fight. Men don't fight.
>> Billy Martin, former manager,
>> before he slugged a Reno sportswriter, 1978

I think, me lads, this is me last slide!
>> King Kelly, former outfielder;
>> his last words as he died of pneumonia, 1894

The termites have got me.
>> Babe Ruth, to a visiting Connie Mack the day
>> before he died of cancer, 1948

I'm all right. Tell Mays not to worry.

> Ray Chapman, Cleveland Indians infielder,
> after getting hit in the head by pitcher Carl Mays in 1920;
> Chapman died the next day

They're hitting me all over the field and I can't get them out.

> Tiny Bonham, Pittsburgh Pirates pitcher;
> his last words as he lay dying after an appendectomy, 1949

I have to get that hit this year. I might die.

> Roberto Clemente, Pittsburgh Pirates outfielder,
> on his 3,000th hit. Clemente was killed in a plane crash
> on December 31, 1972, after finishing the season with
> exactly 3000 hits.

Chapter 13

Fans

---

(1) There is everything to hope for and nothing to fear. (2) Defeats do not disturb one's sleep. (3) An occasional victory is a surprise and a delight. (4) There is no danger of any club passing you, (5) You are not asked fifty times a day, "What was the score?" People take it for granted that you lost.

**Elmer E. Bates, sportswriter,
on the advantages of following a losing team, 1889**

If the crowds get any smaller, they'll have to put fractions on the turnstiles.
Mark Roth, New York Yankees traveling secretary, 1921

Open these for me, will ya, kid? Keep the ones with checks and the ones from the broads. Throw out the others.
**Babe Ruth, New York Yankees outfielder,
throwing his mail to teammate Joe Dugan, 1923**

Oh, hell, who wants to collect that crap?
Babe Ruth, on autographs, 1932

Any ballplayer that don't sign autographs for little kids isn't an American. He's a communist.

Rogers Hornsby, St. Louis Browns infielder

One of the chief duties of the fan is to engage in arguments with the man behind him. This department of the game has been allowed to run down fearfully. **Robert Benchley, writer**

Every time I sign a ball, and there must have been thousands, I thank my luck that I wasn't born Coveleski or Wambaganss or Peckinpaugh. **Mel Ott, New York Giants outfielder, 1948**

The majority of American males put themselves to sleep by striking out the batting order of the New York Yankees.

James Thurber, writer

Knowin' all about baseball is just about as profitable as bein' a good whittler. **Kin Hubbard, humorist**

About this autograph business. Once, someone in Washington sent up a picture to me and I wrote, "Do good in school." I look up, this guy is seventy-eight years old.

Casey Stengel, New York Yankees manager

I love signing autographs. I'll sign anything but veal cutlets. My ballpoint pen slips on veal cutlets. **Casey Stengel**

If the people don't want to come out to the park, nobody's going to stop 'em.

**Yogi Berra, New York Yankees catcher,
on declining attendance in Kansas City**

I seldom refused autograph-seekers, unless they were old enough to look like collection agents.

Joe Pepitone, New York Yankees infielder, 1962

Last year, more Americans went to symphonies than went to baseball games. This may be viewed as an alarming statistic, but I think that both baseball and the country will survive.

John F. Kennedy, 1962

Say this much for big-league baseball—it is beyond question the greatest conversation piece ever invented in America.
Bruce Catton, *New York Herald-Tribune*, 1964

Every player, in his secret heart, wants to manage someday. Every fan, in the privacy of his mind, already does.
Leonard Koppett,
A Thinking Man's Guide to Baseball, 1967

A baseball game is twice as much fun if you're seeing it on the company's time.
William Feather, *The Business of Life*, 1968

I've often wondered what goes into a hot dog. Now I know and I wish I didn't. William Zinsser, *The Lunacy Boom*, 1970

I felt what I almost always feel when I am watching a ball game: Just for those two or three hours, there is really no place I would rather be.
Roger Angell, *The Summer Game*, 1972

Remember, ain't nothing around pleases more than good ball playing. Better than folks has ever seen. They remember it because it *amazes* them. Yeah, it does.
William Brashler,
The Bingo Long Traveling All-Stars and Motor Kings, 1973

I wanted to be a big-league baseball player so I could see my picture on a bubble gum card.
Al Ferrara, Los Angeles Dodgers executive, 1974

Fans don't boo nobodies.
Reggie Jackson, Oakland A's outfielder, 1975

All baseball fans believe in miracles, the question is, how *many* do you believe in? John Updike, novelist

You know, it used to take forty-three Marv Throneberry cards to get one Carl Furillo.
Marv Throneberry, former infielder, 1978

Kids should practice autographing baseballs. This is a skill that's often overlooked in Little League.

Tug McGraw, Philadelphia Phillies pitcher, 1978

As we stand here waiting/For the ball game to start. . . .

Albert Brooks, comic;
his version of "The Star-Spangled Banner," 1978

For some of us, there is a peculiar attraction to baseball. It has its own drama. I have always loved the game. I don't care whether or not it is childish.

James T. Farrell, *The American Scholar*, 1979

Baseball is scrambling for a ball yourself. You don't want an autograph; that's like standing in line for gas.

Bill Lee, Montreal Expos pitcher, 1979

I always wonder if the fans are seeing enough. If you stay with this game and really watch it, your appreciation goes much deeper. It rewards you.

Ted Simmons, St. Louis Cardinals catcher, 1979

Don't worry. The fans don't start booing until July.

Earl Weaver, Baltimore Orioles manager,
to a new manager, 1980

There are surprisingly few real students of the game in baseball, partly because everybody, my eighty-three-year-old mother included, thinks they learned all there was to know about it at puberty. Baseball is very beguiling that way.

Alvin Dark, *When In Doubt, Fire the Manager*, 1980

If they worked as hard at their jobs as I do at mine, this country wouldn't have the inflation problem it has now.

Mike Marshall, Minnesota Twins pitcher,
on booing fans, 1980

I would rather watch baseball played with skill and grace and style than go out myself to ski or play golf or tennis without any of those things. So long as they come to play, I'll happily come to watch.

Art Hill, *I Don't Care If I Never Come Back,* **1980**

We live in a collecting society. Some people collect automobiles or guns, others just collect unemployment.

Bill Lee, Montreal Expos pitcher,
on collecting autographs, 1981

The guy with the biggest stomach will be the first to take off his shirt at a baseball game.

Glenn Dickey, *San Francisco Chronicle,* **1981**

That one little piece of paper—although it may be thrown away an hour later—at that moment was special. The fan and the athlete came together in a personal way.

Steve Garvey, Los Angeles Dodgers infielder,
on autographs, 1981

This is a game to be savored, not gulped. There's time to discuss everything between pitches or between innings.

Bill Veeck, Chicago White Sox owner, 1981

At a Dodger baseball game in Los Angeles, I asked Will Durant if he was ninety-four or ninety-five. "Ninety-four," he said. "You don't think I'd be doing anything as foolish as this if I were ninety-five, do you?"

Norman Cousins, *Human Options,* **1981**

As a nation we are dedicated to keeping physically fit—and parking as close to the stadium as possible.

Bill Vaughn, *Kansas City Star,* **1981**

All baseball fans can be divided into two groups: those who come to batting practice and the others. Only those in the first category have much chance of amounting to anything.

Thomas Boswell, *How Life Imitates the World Series,* **1982**

Baseball, like Pericles' Athens (or any other good society), is simultaneously democratic and aristocratic: Anyone can enjoy it, but the more you apply yourself, the more you enjoy it.

George Will, *Washington Post*, 1982

It is interesting about people that leave early from ball games: It's almost as if they came out to the ball game to see if they can beat the traffic home.

Lon Simmons, Oakland A's announcer, 1982

Chapter 14

Fielding

Get in front of those balls, you won't get hurt. That's what you've got a chest for, young man.

John McGraw, New York Giants manager,
advising third baseman Heinie Groh, 1912

Do not alibi on bad hops; anybody can field the good ones.

Joe McCarthy, New York Yankees manager

Catching a fly ball is a pleasure, but knowing what to do with it after you catch it is a business.

Tommy Henrich, New York Yankees outfielder

There's nothing tough about playing third. All a guy needs is a strong arm and a strong chest.

Frankie Frisch, Pittsburgh Pirates manager

You can shake a tree, and a dozen fielders will fall out.

Branch Rickey, St. Louis Cardinals general manager

Never once did I get hit on the head by a fly ball. Once or twice on the shoulder maybe, but never on the head.

**Babe Herman, former outfielder,
defending his fielding reputation**

I don't like them fellas who drive in two runs and let in three.

Casey Stengel, New York Yankees manager

It gets late early out there.

**Yogi Berra, New York Yankees catcher,
on why the sun makes Yankee Stadium's left field
difficult to play in, October, 1958**

The greatest catch I never made.

**Chuck Hiller, San Francisco Giants infielder,
on a ball stolen out of his glove by Willie Mays, 1961**

We got a guy on our club who has such bad hands his glove is embarrassed.

Frank Sullivan, Philadelphia Phillies pitcher, 1961

Errors are a part of my image.

**Dick "Dr. Strangeglove" Stuart,
Philadelphia Phillies infielder, 1965**

One night in Pittsburgh, thirty thousand fans gave me a standing ovation when I caught a hot-dog wrapper on the fly.

Dick Stuart

Catching a fly ball, or hitting a curved one, is not all that difficult. It may rank in difficulty somewhere below juggling Indian clubs and above playing an ocarina.

Jim Murray, *The Best of Jim Murray*, 1965

If I did anything funny on the ball field it was strictly accidental. Like the way I played third. Some people thought it was hilarious, but I was on the level all the time.

Rocky Bridges, former infielder, 1972

I don't believe it. Lou Brock could never make that play again—not even on instant replay.

Bill Virdon, Pittsburgh Pirates manager,
on a great catch, 1972

Why should I go jackknifing over the fence on my head? That ball has got no business being out there four hundred feet. **Reggie Smith, Los Angeles Dodgers outfielder**

You just plain look like a fool if you drop it. There I was throwing the ball back after the catch, only I didn't have any ball to throw.

Lee Mazzilli, New York Mets outfielder,
on why he gave up the basket catch, 1978

What the hell were you doing last night? Jesus Christ! You looked like a monkey trying to fuck a football out there!

George Steinbrenner, New York Yankees owner,
berating a poor fielder, 1978

If I stay healthy, I have a chance to become the first player ever to collect three thousand hits and one thousand errors.

George Brett, Kansas City Royals infielder, 1979

When you have hands as bad as mine, one hand is better than two.

Ken Harrelson, Cleveland Indians outfielder,
on why he caught balls one-handed, 1979

The poet or storyteller who feels that he is competing with a superb double play in the World Series is a lost man. One would not want as a reader a man who did not appreciate the finesse of a double play.

John Cheever, "In Praise of Readers," 1980

Has anybody ever satisfactorily explained why the bad hop is always the last one?

Hank Greenwald, San Francisco Giants announcer, 1980

I look at it this way. Suppose those thirty pitches had been balls? Then I would have had no errors.

**George Brett, Kansas City Royals infielder,
on his error total for the season, 1980**

Next to the catcher, the third baseman has to be the dumbest guy out there. You can't have any brains to take those shots all day. **Dave Edler, Seattle Mariners infielder, 1981**

When you reach the point when you're too slow to get out of the way, it's time to quit.

Tom Brookens, Detroit Tigers third baseman, 1981

I was playing it like Willie Wilson, but I forgot that I'm in Clint Hurdle's body.

**Clint Hurdle, Kansas City Royals outfielder,
on misplaying a fly ball, 1981**

I was out mowing the lawn during the stike. I got the front yard done, and half the back yard and I kept waiting for Sam Mejias to come out and finish it for me.

**Dave Collins, Cincinnati Reds outfielder,
often taken out for defensive purposes, 1981**

Good stockbrokers are a dime a dozen, but good shortstops are hard to find. **Charles O. Finley, former owner, 1981**

Chapter 15

Hitting and Missing

Keep your eye clear and hit 'em where they ain't.
Wee Willie Keeler, Baltimore Orioles outfielder,
when asked his rules for hitting, 1898

I have seen boys on my baseball teams go into slumps and never come out of them, and I have seen others snap right out and come back better than ever. I guess more players lick themselves than are ever licked by the opposing team.
Connie Mack, Philadelphia Athletics manager and owner

Every great batter works on the theory that the pitcher is more afraid of him than he is of the pitcher.
Ty Cobb, Detroit Tigers outfielder

I had malaria most o' the season. I wound up with .356.
Ring Lardner, "Alibi Ike," 1915

A string of alibis.
Miller Huggins, New York Yankee manager,
asked what a player needs in a slump

A full mind is an empty bat.
> Branch Rickey, St. Louis Cardinals manager

All I can tell 'em is pick a good one and sock it.
> Babe Ruth, New York Yankee outfielder,
> advice to teammates

Scallions are the greatest cure for a batting slump ever invented. **Babe Ruth, eating his way out of a slump, 1934**

How can you think and hit at the same time?
> Yogi Berra, New York Yankees catcher,
> when told he had to think along with the pitcher, 1947

Slump? I ain't in no slump. I just ain't hitting. **Yogi Berra**

Swing at the strikes. **Yogi Berra, advising a batter in a slump**

The art of hitting is the art of getting your pitch to hit.
> Bobby Brown, New York Yankees infielder, 1949

I don't have much confidence in a pinch-hitter no matter who he is. **Jimmy Cannon, *Nobody Asked Me, but . . . , 1951***

I was such a dangerous hitter I even got intentional walks in batting practice. **Casey Stengel, New York Yankees manager**

We've been getting no hits when we got somebody on. Very aggravating. Well, I guess it's better to have somebody left on than not getting on at all. **Casey Stengel**

I ain't up here to read—I'm up here to hit.
> Hank Aaron, Milwaukee Braves outfielder,
> when told his bat label was facing the wrong way, 1957

You wait for a strike. Then you knock the shit out of it.
> Stan Musial, St. Louis Cardinals outfielder,
> when asked how to break out of a slump, 1960

Don't ask me how the baserunners got there. I was asleep in the dugout.

Rod Kanehl, New York Mets infielder,
coming in to pinch-hit, 1962

I coulda hit him. But I wanted to hit him H-A-R-D.

Wes Covington, Philadelphia Phillies outfielder,
explaining why he went down on three strikes

It's a good thing we won one or I'd be eating my heart out. As it is, I'm only eating out my right ventricle.

Ron Swoboda, New York Mets outfielder,
as he struck out five times in a doubleheader, 1969

Boys, bunting is like jacking off. Once you learn how you never forget.   **Joe Schultz, Seattle Pilots manager, 1969**

Everything worthwhile in life is worth a price. Some people give their bodies to science, I give mine to baseball.

Ron Hunt, Montreal Expos infielder,
setting a hit-by-pitch record, 1971

Most managers think pitchers are dumb because we like to do our own thing. Yet we couldn't be too dumb because every year they're changing the rules to make life easier for the hitters.   **Sam McDowell, San Francisco Giants pitcher, 1972**

I can hit buckshot with barbed wire.

George Wilson, Pacific Coast League slugger

Hits just won't come. When you're going like this, it looks like even the umpires have gloves.

Pete Rose, Cincinnati Reds outfielder, 1974

Hitting at 5:15 P.M., with the shadows that are being cast, is like trying to swat flies with a string of spaghetti.

Pete Rose, *Charlie Hustle*, 1974

You know, this game's not very much fun when you're only hitting .247. Reggie Jackson, Oakland A's outfielder, 1975

I'm nothing for August.
> Lee May, Baltimore Orioles outfielder

Take your bat with you.
> Earl Weaver, Baltimore Orioles manager,
> to a slump-ridden Al Bumbry on his way to chapel, 1979

I'm the only man in the history of the game who began his career in a slump and stayed in it.
> Rocky Bridges, former infielder, 1973

I was the worst hitter ever. I never even broke a bat until last year. Then I was backing out of the garage.
> Lefty Gomez, former pitcher, 1975

You don't always *make* an out. Sometimes the pitcher *gets* you out. Carl Yastrzemski, Boston Red Sox outfielder, 1978

How hard is hitting? You ever walk into a pitch-black room full of furniture that you've never been in before and try to walk through it without bumping into anything? Well, it's harder than that. Ted Kluszewski, former infielder, 1978

If you don't swing at bad pitches, they have to throw you a good one. Gates Brown, Detroit Tigers coach, 1979

When you take a pitch and *line* it somewhere, it's like you've thought of something and put it with beautiful clarity.
> Reggie Jackson, New York Yankees outfielder, 1979

You decide you'll wait for your pitch. Then as the ball starts toward the plate, you think about your stance. And then you think about your swing. And then you realize that the ball that went past you for a strike was your pitch.
> Bobby Murcer, New York Yankees outfielder,
> on slumps, 1980

Each time I was in a slump it seemed like I'd have to go out and face a Drysdale, a Koufax, or a Marichal that particular afternoon. It never failed.

Billy Williams, former outfielder, 1980

I got the sophomore jinx out of the way and I think I'll have my best year ever next year. There's no junior jinx, is there?

Joe Charboneau, Cleveland Indians outfielder, 1981

Don't worry about hitting from that side. I've got that side taken care of.

**Cliff Johnson, Oakland A's designated hitter,
to a switch-hitting rookie, 1981**

It was a low fastball. It just happened to be right where I was swinging.

**Alan Ashby, Houston Astros catcher,
on what he hit for a home run, 1981**

Either it was the best he's ever thrown against us or the worst we've ever swung.

**Bill Madlock, Pittsburgh Pirates infielder,
on a Mike LaCoss shutout, 1981**

Sure, I screwed up that sacrifice bunt, but look at it this way. I'm a better bunter than a billion Chinese. Those poor suckers can't bunt at all.

John Lowenstein, Baltimore Orioles outfielder, 1981

I flush the john between innings to keep my wrists strong.

**John Lowenstein,
on how he stays warm as a designated hitter, 1981**

Damn, I'm going so bad that I don't even get thrown out of the game right. Aren't they supposed to give you a chance to stand around and argue?

Oscar Gamble, New York Yankees outfielder, 1981

I'm trying to get down to zero and start the season over.
Dave Lopes, Los Angeles Dodgers infielder,
hitting under .100, 1981

If you have a batting slump or a cold, you will get plenty of advice. Chicken soup certainly isn't going to cure a batting slump.
Hank Greenwald, San Francisco Giants announcer, 1981

Not many people talk to you when you're hitting .195.
Dwight Evans, Boston Red Sox outfielder,
asked if he got any advice on his slump, 1981

You know you're going bad when your wife takes you aside and tries to change your batting stance. And you take her advice.

Thomas Boswell,
How Life Imitates the World Series, 1982

What makes a good pinch hitter? I wish to hell I knew.
Bobby Murcer, New York Yankees outfielder, 1982

Chapter 16

Home Runs

That score board ain't for you to look at. It's for you to hit that old pill against.

**Ring Lardner, a manager advising a
player in his story, "Alibi Ike," 1915**

A homer a day will boost my pay.

Josh Gibson, Negro-leagues catcher, 1930

Hell, I could have hit .600 myself! But I'm paid to hit homers.
Babe Ruth, New York Yankees outfielder, to Ty Cobb

Cadillacs are down at the end of the bat.

**Ralph Kiner, Pittsburgh Pirates outfielder,
when asked why he didn't choke up and hit for average**

I never saw a fucking ball get out of a fucking ball park so fucking fast in my fucking life.

**Leo Durocher, New York Giants manager,
on Willie Mays' titanic first major-league home run, 1951**

For the first sixty feet it was a hell of a pitch.

> **Warren Spahn, Boston Braves pitcher,**
> **on what he threw for Mays' homer, 1951**

It was a month of Sundays.

> **Red Smith, on Bobby Thomson's pennant-clinching**
> **home run for the New York Giants,**
> *New York Herald-Tribune*, **1951**

That's the first time I've seen a big fat wallet go flying into the seats.

> **Clyde Sukeforth, Brooklyn Dodgers pitcher,**
> **on Bobby Thomson's "shot heard 'round the world," 1951**

Why me? I don't smoke. I don't drink. I don't run around. Baseball is my whole life. Why me?

> **Ralph Branca, Brooklyn Dodgers pitcher,**
> **to a priest after Thomson hit the his-**
> **toric home run off him, 1951**

The greatest thrill in the world is to end the game with a home run and watch everybody else walk off the field while you're running the bases on air.

> **Al Rosen, Cleveland Indians infielder**

One long ball hitter, that's what we need. I'd sell my soul for one long ball hitter—hey, where did you come from?

> **Robert Shafer, Senators manager,**
> **encountering the devil in *Damn Yankees*,**
> **a play by Douglas Wallop and George Abbott, 1958**

It's my job to hit a home run. You don't have to shake my hand for doing my job.

> **Alex Johnson, California Angels outfielder, 1970**

I hit one that far once. I did. And I still bogeyed the hole.

> **Ron Fairly, Montreal Expos outfielder,**
> **on a Mike Schmidt home run off the speakers**
> **on the Astrodome roof, 1973**

God, do I love to hit that little round sum-bitch out of the park and make 'em say "Wow!"
Reggie Jackson, Oakland A's outfielder, 1974

It was an insurance run, so I hit it to the Prudential Building.
Reggie Jackson, on a home run in Boston

I looked in my glove and then on the ground. That left only one place—the other side of the fence.
Pat Kelly, Baltimore Orioles outfielder,
on how he knew a batter had hit a home run, 1977

I wanted to go into my home-run trot, but then I realized I didn't have one.
Jim Essian, Chicago White Sox catcher,
on his first major-league home run, 1977

You hit home runs by not trying to hit home runs. I know that doesn't sound right, and it won't *read* right, but that's the way it is.   **Charley Lau, Kansas City Royals coach, 1978**

As I remember it, the bases were loaded.
Garry Maddox, Philadelphia Phillies outfielder,
asked about his grand-slam home run, 1979

Reggie Jackson hit one off me that's still burrowing its way to Los Angeles.
Dan Quisenberry, Kansas City Royals pitcher, 1981

When you don't hit too many home runs, you just run until somebody catches it.
Dave Bergman, San Francisco Giants infielder,
asked if he knew he ball he hit was gone, 1981

What's one home run? If you hit one, they are just going to want you to hit two.
Mick Kelleher, Detroit Tigers infielder,
homerless in a ten-year career, 1981

The key to winning baseball games is pitching, fundamentals and three-run homers.

Earl Weaver, Baltimore Orioles manager, 1982

Chapter 17

Infielders

Richie Allen (1963–77)

Your body is just like a bar of soap. It gradually wears down from repeated use.

Richie Allen, on why he took things easy, 1968

Play him, fine him, and play him again.

Gene Mauch, former Philadelphia Phillies manager, on how to handle Allen, 1982

Luke Appling (1930–50)

When Appling was around, the real blunder was to ask him, "How do you feel?" It would sometimes take half an hour before he stopped telling you.

Maury Allen, *Big-Time Baseball*, 1978

Ernie Banks (1953–71)

Without Ernie Banks, the Cubs would finish in Albuquerque.
Jimmy Dykes, Cincinnati Reds manager, 1958

He never remembered a sign or forgot a newspaperman's name. **Leo Durocher, Chicago Cubs manager, 1975**

Ernie Banks is the only person who would have been happy to be here.
Oscar Gamble, New York Yankees outfielder, on the club under George Steinbrenner, 1982

Moe Berg (1923–39)

He could speak eight languages, but he couldn't hit in any of them. **Ted Lyons, Chicago White Sox pitcher**

Yogi Berra (1946–65)

He isn't much to look at, and he looks like he's doing everything wrong, but he can hit. He got a couple of hits off us on wild pitches.
Mel Ott, New York Giants manager, advising Horace Stoneham, 1946

YANKEE TEAM KILLED IN PLANE CRASH
BERRA LIVES—CATCHES LATER FLIGHT
Jim Bouton, New York Yankees pitcher, fantasizing a newspaper headline on Berra's luck

Not only is he lucky, he's never wrong.
Whitey Ford, New York Yankees pitcher

Yeah, but I defy anybody to throw him a good ball.
Hal Newhouser, Detroit Tigers pitcher, when told Yogi was a bad-ball hitter

Yogi was Mr. Straight, Mr. America, Mr. White Underwear.
**Howard Levine, advertising executive,
on why he wanted Yogi for a commercial**

He ain't sleeping, he's just thinking about money.
Casey Stengel

He's one of those Christmas Eve guys. There are people like
that. . . . Every day in their lives is Christmas Eve
Joe Garagiola, broadcaster, 1974

Yogi's face is his fortune.
Fred Stanley, New York Yankees infielder

Lou Boudreau (1938–52)

He is easily the slowest ballplayer since Ernie Lombardi was
thrown out at first base trying to stretch a double into a
single. **Stanley Frank, sportswriter**

George Brett (1973–   )

The only way to pitch him is inside, so you force him to pull
the ball. That way, the line drive won't hit you.
Rudy May, New York Yankees pitcher, 1980

I tell him, "Attaway to hit, George."
**Jim Frey, Kansas City Royals manager,
his hitting advice to Brett, 1980**

George is getting to be such a monster that I'd hate to die
in a car wreck with the guy. You'd be listed as: Others Killed.
Clint Hurdle, Kansas City Royals outfielder, 1981

Bobby Brown (1946–54)

Bobby Brown reminds me of a fellow who's been hitting for
twelve years and fielding one.
Casey Stengel, New York Yankees manager, 1952

Rick Burleson (1974–)

He's even-tempered. He comes to the ball park mad and stays
that way.

> Joe Garagiola, broadcaster,
> on Burleson's aggressiveness, 1981

Dolph Camilli (1933–45)

Nobody knew how well Dolph could fight because, quite
frankly, nobody had ever wanted to find out.

> Leo Durocher, *Nice Guys Finish Last*, 1975

Chris Cannizzaro (1960–74)

He's a remarkable catcher, that Canzoneri. He's the only defensive catcher in baseball who can't catch.

> Casey Stengel, New York Mets manager, 1966

Rod Carew (1967–)

He can't miss. If I were him I'd go looking for wallets.

> Jerry McNertney, Seattle Pilots catcher, 1969

He has an uncanny ability to move the ball around as if the
bat were some kind of magic wand.

> Ken Holtzman, Chicago Cubs pitcher, 1970

He's the only guy I know who can go four for three.

> Alan Bannister, Chicago White Sox infielder, 1976

Watching Rod Carew bat is like watching Bulova make a
watch, DeBeers cut a diamond. . . . Rod Carew doesn't make
hits, he composes them.

> Jim Murray, *Los Angeles Times*, 1979

Carew babies his batting average with the tender care of an
orchid gardener.

> Blackie Sherrod, *Philadelphia Inquirer*, 1979

Choo Choo Coleman (1961–66)

He is quick on the base paths, but this is an attribute that is about as essential for catchers as neat handwriting.

Roger Angell, *Late Innings,* **1982**

Billy Cox (1941–55)

That ain't a third baseman. That's a fucking acrobat.

Casey Stengel, New York Yankees manager

Babe Dahlgren (1935–46)

His arms are too short. He makes easy plays look hard.

Joe McCarthy, New York Yankees manager, 1940

Nick Etten (1938–47)

Nick Etten's glove fields better with Nick Etten out of it.

Joe Trimble, Pittsburgh Pirates pitcher, 1952

Jimmy Foxx (1925–45)

I was pitching one day, when my glasses clouded up on me. I took them off to polish them. When I looked up the plate, I saw Jimmy Foxx. The sight of him terrified me so much that I haven't been able to wear glasses since.

Lefty Gomez, New York Yankees pitcher

He once started a restaurant and showed up for the grand opening four days late.

Bill Veeck, Chicago White Sox owner, 1981

Steve Garvey (1969–   )

Garvey is the only first baseman who washes his glove.

Don Rickles, comic, 1979

Everything about him is neat. He's the pinnacle of what everyone should be. Really, isn't that awful? It makes life so boring.

> Cynthia Garvey, wife, 1980

Anybody who has plastic hair is bound to have problems.

> Jay Johnstone, Los Angeles Dodgers outfielder, 1981

Lou Gehrig (1923–39)

I'm not a headline guy. I know that as long as I was following Ruth to the plate I could have stood on my head and no one would have known the difference. Lou Gehrig, 1927

Hell, Lou, it took fifteen years to get you out of the game. Sometimes I'm out in fifteen minutes.

> Lefty Gomez, New York Yankees pitcher,
> to Gehrig, who sat down after playing
> 2130 consecutive games, 1939

Today I consider myself the luckiest man on the face of the earth. I might have been given a bad break, but I've got an awful lot to live for. Thank you.

> Lou Gehrig, in a speech at Yankee Stadium,
> when he was dying of a rare disease, 1939

He was the guy who hit all those home runs the year Ruth broke the record. Franklin P. Adams, columnist, 1948

Gehrig had one advantage over me. He was a better ballplayer.

> Gil Hodges, Brooklyn Dodgers infielder,
> when he was compared to Gehrig, 1962

Charlie Gehringer (1924–42)

He'd say hello at the start of spring training and goodbye at the end of the season, and the rest of the time he let his bat and glove do all the talking for him.

> Ty Cobb, Detroit Tigers outfielder

Charlie Gehringer is in a rut. He hits .350 on opening day and stays there all season.

Lefty Gomez, New York Yankees pitcher

Josh Gibson (Negro leagues, 1927–45)

You look for his weakness and while you lookin' for it, he liable to hit forty-five home runs.

Satchel Paige, Negro-leagues pitcher

He could hit any pitch to any field. The only way to pitch to him was to throw the ball low and behind him.

Chet Brewer, Negro-leagues pitcher

Gibson was, at the minimum, two Yogi Berras.

Bill Veeck, former owner, 1982

Greg Goosen (1965–70)

I got a kid, Greg Goosen, he's nineteen years old and in ten years he's got a chance to be twenty-nine.

Casey Stengel, New York Mets manager, on Goosen's potential, 1965

Mike Hargrove (1974–)

I feel my ability as a ballplayer is overshadowed by people saying: "Hey, look at that idiot at the plate."

Mike Hargrove, who takes so long at the plate that he is called the "Human Rain Delay," 1981

He's a one-man four-corner offense.

Doc Medich, Texas Rangers pitcher, 1982

Bob Horner (1978–   )

You know how the fans in the left-field stands will gather and wait for the home-run ball to come down? Well, he hit the ball so hard they scattered.

Frank LaCorte, Houston Astros pitcher, 1981

Plan A didn't work, and I'm abandoning it and going to Plan B.

**Don Sutton, Houston Astros pitcher,
on how he pitches to Horner, 1981**

Rogers Hornsby (1915–37)

He was frank to the point of being cruel, and subtle as a belch.   **Lee Allen, baseball historian**

Elston Howard (1955–68)

When I finally get a nigger, I get the only one in the world who can't run.

Casey Stengel, New York Yankees manager, 1955

Randy Hundley (1964–77)

Having Hundley catch for you was like sitting down to a steak dinner with a steak knife. Without Hundley all you had was a fork.   **Ferguson Jenkins, Chicago Cubs pitcher, 1970**

Mike Ivie (1971–   )

Mike Ivie is a forty-million-dollar airport with a thirty-dollar control tower.

Rick Monday, Los Angeles Dodgers outfielder, 1981

I don't have much of a personality. If they paid you on the basis of your personality, I'd make about two dollars a year.

Mike Ivie, 1981

Hughie Jennings (1891–1918)

There was nothing sedate about Hughie. He once survived a running dive into a concrete swimming pool—after the pool had been unexpectedly drained.

Ty Cobb, Detroit Tigers outfielder

Harvey Kuenn (1952–66)

If the guy was hurt, his team might be hurt, but the pitching all over the league will improve.

Casey Stengel, New York Yankees manager, 1960

Jerry Lumpe (1956–67)

He looks like the greatest hitter in the world till you play him.

Casey Stengel, New York Yankees manager, 1959

Willie McCovey (1959–80)

On ground balls hit down to the second baseman, there's no need to throw, the second baseman just hands it to Willie.

Jim Murray, *Los Angeles Times*

Frank Malzone (1955–66)

The guy's got a fault? Dandruff, maybe.

Leo Durocher, New York Giants manager, 1955

Rabbit Maranville (1912–35)

He picked a fight with a cabbie and lost. He fought three more of them, and they all beat the hell out of him. So I asked him what he was doing. He said: "I'm trying to find one I can whip."

Bill Veeck, Chicago White Sox owner, 1981

Pepper Martin (1928–44)

Pepper goes out on the prairie and scares up a bunch of rabbits. He runs along with these rabbits, and reaches down and feels their sides. If the rabbit is a bit thin he lets them go.
Roy Moore, minor-league pitcher, 1928

A chunky, unshaven hobo who ran the bases like a beserk locomotive, slept in the raw, and swore at pitchers in his sleep.
Lee Allen, *The National League Story*, 1961

John Mayberry (1968–   )

Big John is so nice and easy-going you don't suspect anything when he asks you to take your foot off the bag to kick the dust away—until he tags you.
Bobby Grich, California Angels infielder, 1981

Johnny Mize (1936–53)

Before each game an announcement is made that anyone interfering with or touching a batted ball will be ejected from the park. Please advise Mr. Mize that this doesn't apply to him.
Goodman Ace, writer, wire to Leo Durocher, 1948

Joe Morgan (1963–   )

Joe, it's funny how all these winning teams seem to follow you around. **Bill Russell, former basketball player, 1981**

Graig Nettles (1967–   )

They call him "Puff" because he's always provoking fights, then when they start, *puff*, he's gone.
Joe Garagiola, broadcaster, 1977

If we'd known he wanted a car so bad, we'd have given it to him.

**Johnny Bench, Cincinnati Reds catcher,
on Nettles winning the World Series MVP award, 1978**

Talk about somebody able to catch bullets with his teeth: Maybe Nettles can.

Lon Simmons, Oakland A's announcer, 1981

Joe Pepitone (1962–73)

He was playing in Japan. The last I heard he wasn't happy there, either. The Japanese people were very inconsiderate. They insisted upon speaking Japanese.

Leo Durocher, *Nice Guys Finish Last*, 1975

He was known to play night games no matter what it said on the schedule. **Vic Ziegel, *Inside Sports*, 1981**

Tony Perez (1964–)

How can anyone who runs as slow as you pull a muscle?

Pete Rose, Cincinnati Reds outfielder, 1974

Paul Popovich (1964–75)

Sit down, Paul. We ain't giving up yet.

**Leo Durocher, Chicago Cubs manager,
when Popovich rose to go into the game, 1966**

Boog Powell (1961–77)

If he held out his arm, he'd be a railroad crossing.

Joe Garagiola, broadcaster

Jerry Remy (1975–   )

The A's need a hit or a Boston mistake. If they are looking for a Boston mistake, I suggest they don't hit it to Remy.
                    Lon Simmons, Oakland A's broadcaster, 1981

Bobby Richardson (1955–65)

Look at him. He doesn't drink, he doesn't smoke, he doesn't chew, he doesn't stay out late, and he still can't hit .250.
                    Casey Stengel, New York Mets manager

Phil Rizzuto (1941–56)

My best pitch is anything the batter grounds, lines or pops in the direction of Rizzuto.
                    Vic Raschi, New York Yankees pitcher

Brooks Robinson (1955–71)

Brooks Robinson belongs in a Higher League.
                    Pete Rose, Cincinnati Reds outfielder,
                    after Robinson's sensational World Series, 1970

He's not at his locker yet, but four guys are over there interviewing his glove.
                    Rex Barney, Baltimore Orioles coach, to reporters trying
                    to interview Robinson after the World Series, 1970

Brooks never asked anyone to name a candy bar after him. In Baltimore, people name their children after him.
                    Gordon Beard, sportswriter, 1973

He charged everything. He reacted as the ball was coming off the bat, sometimes as it was coming *to* the bat.
                    George Brett, Kansas City Royals infielder, 1981

Jackie Robinson (1947–56)

There was never a man in the game who could put mind and muscle together quicker and with better judgement than Robinson. **Branch Rickey, Brooklyn Dodgers president**

Pete Rose (1963–)

Does Pete hustle? Before the All-Star Game he came into the clubhouse and took off his shoes—and they ran another mile without him. **Hank Aaron, Atlanta Braves outfielder, 1973**

He can brainwash me from sixty feet away. . . . He sets up pitchers the way pitchers try to set up Pete Rose.
Tug McGraw, *Screwball*, 1974

He gets base hits in the present and lives in the past. He should be dancing the Charleston, drinking sarsaparilla, and wearing a big-brimmed fedora.
Larry Merchant, *Ringside Seat at the Circus*, 1976

Pete doesn't run with celebrities. He can't stand phonies. His big buddy in L.A. ain't Sinatra. It's a funny old groundskeeper. **Sparky Anderson, Detroit Tigers manager, 1979**

Walk by a house that's being built, stop awhile and watch the bricklayers. Pretty soon you'll be able to tell who is the best bricklayer by his drive, his determination. Pete has more drive within him. He's the best bricklayer out there.
Willie Stargell, Pittsburgh Pirates infielder, 1979

He is what Norman Rockwell would draw for a *Saturday Evening Post* cover if he was doing a ballplayer. Pete looks as if he should have a dog with him.
Jim Murray, *Los Angeles Times*, 1980

Rose wishes he was a wide receiver so he could spike the ball.
Clint Hurdle, Kansas City Royals outfielder, 1981

Pete Rose is the most likeable arrogant person I've ever met.
Mike Schmidt, Philadelphia Phillies infielder, 1981

I'd walk through hell in a gasoline suit to keep playing baseball. **Pete Rose, 1981**

Manny Sanguillen (1967–1981)

The way to fool Manny Sanguillen is to throw him right down the middle. He'll hit anything but a perfect pitch.
Billy DeMars, Philadelphia Phillies batting coach, 1978

Steve Sax (1981–)

He plays baseball like my wife shops—all day long.
Tom Lasorda, Los Angeles Dodgers manager, 1981

We tell him: "Hey, slow down. After you touch home plate there is no other base to run to."
Rick Monday, Los Angeles Dodgers outfielder, 1982

Ted Simmons (1968–)

He didn't sound like a baseball player. He said things like "Nevertheless," and "If, in fact."
Dan Quisenberry, Kansas City Royals pitcher, 1981

Moose Skowron (1954–67)

The way he's going I'd be better off if he was hurt.
Casey Stengel, New York Mets manager

Eddie Stanky (1943–53)

Stanky couldn't hit, couldn't run, couldn't field and couldn't throw, but was still the best player on the club. All Mr. Stanky could do for you was *win*.
Branch Rickey, Brooklyn Dodgers president, 1945

Garry Templeton (1976–   )

He doesn't want to play in St. Louis. He doesn't want to play on turf. He doesn't want to play when we go into Montreal. He doesn't want to play in the Astrodome. He doesn't want to play in the rain. The other eighty games he's all right.

Whitey Herzog, St. Louis Cardinals manager, 1981

Bill Terry (1923–36)

Could be that he's a nice guy when you get to know him, *but why bother?* **Dizzy Dean, St. Louis Cardinals pitcher**

He once hit a ball between my legs so hard that my center fielder caught it on the fly backing up against the wall.

Dizzy Dean

Terry, you can ask for more money in the winter and do less in the summer than any ballplayer I know.

John McGraw, New York Giants manager

Marv Throneberry (1955–63)

We was going to get you a birthday cake, but we figured you'd drop it. **Casey Stengel, New York Mets manager, 1962**

How could he be expected to remember where the bases were? He gets on so infrequently.

Jack Lang, sportswriter, after Throneberry was called out for missing first base, 1962

Marv got the Good Guy award mixed up with the Most Valuable Player award.

George Weiss, New York Mets executive, after Throneberry held out on his contract, 1963

Marvelous Marv was holding down first base. This is like saying Willie Sutton works at your bank.

Jimmy Breslin,
***Can't Anybody Here Play This Game?*, 1963**

All Murph or I had to say was, "Throneberry drops it," and Mets fans back home fell out of their seats laughing.

Lindsey Nelson, New York Mets announcer, 1965

Bob Uecker (1962–67)

I was only in the majors two months before I got a raise. The minimum went up. **Bob Uecker, 1977**

Reggie Jackson wouldn't get into the batter's box until he knew we were back from commercial. Of course, Uecker wanted to hit *during* the commercial.

Al Michaels, sportscaster, 1982

Honus Wagner (1897–1917)

That goddamn Dutchman is the only man in the game I can't scare. **Ty Cobb, Detroit Tigers outfielder**

The way to get a ball past Honus is to hit it eight feet over his head! **John McGraw, New York Giants manager**

Pete Ward (1962–70)

I'd make him a catcher, but we'd never get the game over with. He'd use up the whole night gossiping with the hitters and umpires. **Al Lopez, Chicago White Sox manager, 1965**

Chapter 18

Labor

Us ballplayers stick together like a wishbone in a pulling contest. **Arthur "Bugs" Baer,** *Collier's,* **1942**

I just didn't want to go to Philadelphia. It was a selfish thing, really.

Curt Flood,
on why he challenged the reserve clause, 1971

I don't need an agent. Why should I give somebody ten percent when I do all the work?

Mark Fidrych, Detroit Tigers pitcher, 1976

If you tell enough people in a press box your client played a great game, some will write it, whether he did or not.

Bob Woolf, agent, 1977

When they smile, blood drips off their teeth.

Ted Turner, Atlanta Braves owner, on agents, 1978

We're doing this whole thing backward. Attorneys should wear numbers on their backs, and box scores should have entries for writs, depositions and appeals.

Bill Veeck, Chicago White Sox owner, 1978

They all changed. Most of them got agents, and I ceased to talk to 'em. "Like to use this toilet paper?" "Dunno, I gotta talk to my agent."

Bill Lee, Montreal Expos pitcher, on today's players, 1979

A complete ballplayer today is one who can hit, field, run, throw and pick the right agent.

Bob Lurie, San Francisco Giants owner, 1981

When I negotiated Bob Stanley's contract with the Red Sox, we had statistics demonstrating he was the third-best pitcher in the league. They had a chart showing he was the sixth-best pitcher on the Red Sox. **Bob Woolf, agent, 1981**

If everyone contributes what their agents say they'll contribute, we'll have 172 wins and no losses.

Dave Garcia, Cleveland Indians manager, 1981

I knew I was in trouble when the arbitrator asked what we meant by such symbols as IP, BB and ERA.

Greg Minton, San Francisco Giants pitcher, 1981

The pitchers tomorrow? Well, just say Marvin Miller against Ray Grebey.

Hank Greenwald, San Francisco Giants announcer, on the bargaining representatives the day before the strike, 1981

Those ballplayers better talk to some auto workers and steelworkers. Good Japanese ballplayers can be imported, too.

Martha Cummins, on the strike, *Houston Post*, 1981

The Cubs striking is about as significant as the buggy-whip manufacturers going on strike. What difference does it make?

Mike Royko, *Chicago Sun-Times*, 1981

I don't think baseball is real life. But strikes are real life. It took up seven weeks of real time. That's a fifth of a pregnancy.
Dan Quisenberry, Kansas City Royals pitcher, 1981

I think what we've created here is a concrete glider.
**Roy Eisenhardt, Oakland A's president,
on the complicated free-agency plan adopted
to end the strike, 1981**

Attendance is back up. There are a lot of kids born in the last year who didn't know about the strike and are coming to the games. **Bob Uecker, Milwaukee Brewers announcer, 1982**

Chapter 19

Leisure and Travel

Leisure is the handmaiden of the devil.
Branch Rickey, St. Louis Cardinals general manager

Them goddamn squirrels running in and outta trees. They're killing my game. Get me an air rifle.
Babe Ruth, New York Yankees outfielder, playing golf,
before he attacked the offending animals, 1927

When I hit a ball, I want someone else to go chase it.
Rogers Hornsby, St. Louis Cardinals infielder, on golf

The road will make a bum out of the best of them.
Harold Rosenthal, baseball writer

I usually take a two-hour nap, from one o'clock to four.
Yogi Berra, New York Yankees catcher,
on how he spends his time before a night game

Come over here and show me how to work this thing!
Yogi Berra, calling a teammate about his new piano

I heard that actors start work at six o'clock in the morning. That sort of soured me on the whole thing.

Bo Belinsky, Los Angeles Angels pitcher

All the time it's fasten your goddamn seatbelt. But how come every time I read about one of those plane crashes, there's 180 people on board and all 180 die? Didn't any of them have their seatbelt fastened?

Fred Talbot, Seattle Pilots pitcher, 1969

Damn, if this plane goes down I hope the newspapers at least have me listed in the probable starting pitchers.

Jim Bouton, Houston Astros pitcher, during a bumpy flight, 1969

In baseball you hit a home run over the right-field fence, the left-field fence, the center-field fence. Nobody cares. In golf everything has got to be right over second base.

Ken Harrelson, Cleveland Indians infielder

He who have the fastest cart never have to play bad lie.

Mickey Mantle, former outfielder, on golf, 1971

The pay is great, and the only way you can get hurt playing golf is by getting struck by lightning.

Ted Williams, former outfielder, on professional golf, 1972

We're going down. We're going down and I have a .300 life-time average to take with me. Do you?

Pete Rose, Cincinnati Reds outfielder, to his airplane seatmate Hal King, 1974

I'd do much better if they'd build golf courses in a circle. You see, I have this slice.

Rocky Bridges, Triple-A Hawaii Islanders manager, 1972

It took me seventeen years to get three thousand hits in baseball. I did it in one afternoon on the golf course.

Hank Aaron, former outfielder, 1978

Some of our guys don't know what to do with the free time. I suggested they go to San Francisco. They said, "What is there to do there?"   **Brian Kingman, Oakland A's pitcher, 1981**

Going to the theater [to a ballplayer] means lying in an un-made hotel bed and slurping a can of Lite Beer, while he watches "As the World Turns."

Lowell Cohn, *San Francisco Chronicle*, 1981

Chapter 20

Macho

Sportsmanship and easygoing methods are all right, but it is the prospect of a hot fight that brings out the crowds.
John McGraw, New York Giants manager

I couldn't make any headway against him talking.
Rogers Hornsby, St. Louis Cardinals manager,
on why he socked rival manager Art Fletcher, 1925

When Mr. Billy Martin and Mr. Mickey Mantle came to me they were such kids in their hotel rooms they were having pretend gun fights with toy guns, which they would draw on each other and then argue who was the fastest on the draw.
Casey Stengel, New York Yankees manager

How about that tag?
Eddie Matthews, Milwaukee Braves infielder,
socking Frank Robinson after Robinson
complained about a hard tag

Where I come from we just talk for a little while. After that we start to hit.   **Gene Brabender, Seattle Pilots pitcher, 1969**

There's not a guy living who ever saw me rub.
Al Rosen, former infielder, 1972

I took your best shot right on the elbow, you big donkey, and I'm still playing. [signed] The White Gorilla.
Thurman Munson, New York Yankees catcher,
wiring pitcher Goose Gossage after being hit, 1976

I clocked them. There are two guys in this town looking for their teeth.
George Steinbrenner, New York Yankees owner,
after his fight in a Los Angeles elevator
during the World Series, 1981

If they try to knock you over, hit the motherfucker right in the mouth with the ball.
Billy Martin, New York Yankees manager,
to a rookie catcher, 1978

I don't throw the first punch. I throw the second four.
Billy Martin, Oakland A's manager, 1981

I'm not sure what it means, but whenever the ball is not in play, somebody grabs his crotch.
Paula Bouton, wife of former pitcher Jim Bouton,
trying to figure out baseball, 1981

Chapter 21

Managing

Sometimes I think I'm in the greatest business in the world. Then you lose four straight and want to change places with the farmer. **Joe McCarthy, New York Yankees manager**

Just hold them for a few innings, fellas. I'll think of something.
Charlie Dressen, Brooklyn Dodgers manager

Tell a ballplayer something a thousand times, then tell him again, because that might be the time he'll understand something. **Paul Richards, Baltimore Orioles manager**

It ain't like football. You can't make up no trick plays.
**Yogi Berra, New York Yankees manager,
asked if he had new plans for the World Series, 1964**

What do managers *really* do? Worry. Constantly. For a living.
Leonard Koppett, *A Thinking Man's Guide to Baseball*, 1967

Run everything out and be in by twelve.
                    Red Schoendienst, St. Louis Cardinals manager,
                                    to his players, 1968

The manager was fired twice, but was hired again on the
grounds that he's a sound baseball man. A sound baseball man
is anybody who has been fired twice.
                    Leonard Shecter, *The Jocks*, 1970

There are three things the average man thinks he can do better than anybody else: build a fire, run a hotel and manage a
baseball team.
          Rocky Bridges, manager, Triple-A San Jose Bees, 1972

I'm not concerned about the other team stealing my signs.
I'm just concerned about us getting them.
          Frank Howard, manager, Triple-A Spokane Indians, 1976

Most managers are lifetime .220 hitters. For years, pitchers
have been getting those managers out seventy-five percent of
the time, and that's why they don't like us.
                    Bill Lee, Montreal Expos pitcher, 1979

Each year, new managers appear. And each season, the public
response is "Who's he? Why him?" The fans never catch on.
They want John Wayne and Humphrey Bogart. But they keep
getting Jim Frey and Dick Howser.
                    Thomas Boswell, *Inside Sports*, 1980

I never play by The Book because I've never met the guy who
wrote it.   **Dick Williams, Montreal Expos manager, 1980**

You just listen to the ball and bat come together. They make
an awful noise.
                    Darrell Johnson, Seattle Mariners manager,
                            on when to change pitchers, 1980

The worse thing is the day you realize you want to win more
than the players do.
                    Gene Mauch, Minnesota Twins manager, 1980

When we lost I couldn't sleep at night. When we win I can't sleep at night. But when you win, you wake up feeling better.
Joe Torre, New York Mets manager, 1980

I think they recycle more managers than cans.
Bill North, San Francisco Giants outfielder, 1981

The toughest thing for me as a younger manager is the fact that a lot of these guys saw me play. So it's hard for me to instruct them in anything, because they know how bad I was.
Tony LaRussa, Chicago White Sox manager and lifetime .199 hitter, 1981

Most pitchers are too smart to manage.
Jim Palmer, Baltimore Orioles pitcher, on why so few pitchers became managers, 1981

The pilgrims didn't have any experience when they first arrived here. Hell, if experience was that important, we'd never have had anybody walking on the moon.
Doug Rader, former infielder, wanting to become a manager, 1981

Managers really encouraged players to talk it up on the bench. That was important. You had to keep those guys from falling asleep, because I've seen guys fall right off that bench and onto the disabled list. **Bob Feller, former pitcher, 1981**

Walter Alston (Brooklyn Dodgers and Los Angeles Dodgers, 1954–76)

You know Walt Alston. The only guy in the game who could look Billy Graham right in the eye without blushing, who would order corn on the cob in a Paris restaurant.
Jim Murray, *The Best of Jim Murray*, 1965

Sparky Anderson (Cincinati Reds and Detroit Tigers, 1970–)

Me carrying a briefcase is like a hog wearing earrings.
Sparky Anderson, 1979

I refuse to call a forty-seven-year-old man Sparky.

Al Clark, umpire,
on why he calls Anderson "George," 1981

Sparky came here two years ago promising to build a team in his own image, and now the club is looking for small, white-haired infielders with .212 batting averages.

Al Ackerman, Detroit sportscaster, 1981

Players have two things to do: Play and keep their mouths shut. **Sparky Anderson, 1982**

He really believes that he made a winning team out of Pete Rose, Johnny Bench, Joe Morgan, George Foster and Davey Concepcion by teaching them the virtues of shiny shoes and clean upper lips. **Bill James, *Sport*, 1982**

Alvin Dark (San Francisco Giants, Kansas City Athletics, Cleveland Indians, Oakland A's, and San Diego Padres, 1961–77)

I knew Alvin Dark was a religious man, but he's worshipping the wrong god—Charles O. Finley.

Vida Blue, Oakland A's pitcher, 1974

Leo Durocher (Brooklyn Dodgers, New York Giants, Chicago Cubs, and Houston Astros, 1939–73)

He had the the ability of taking a bad situation and making it immediately worse.

Branch Rickey, Brooklyn Dodgers president

You and Durocher are on a raft. A wave comes and knocks him into the ocean. You dive in and save his life. A shark comes and takes your leg. Next day, you and Leo start out even.

Dick Young, sportswriter

Leo would play a convicted rapist if he could turn the double play.

Jim Bouton, *I Managed Good,*
***But Boy Did They Play Bad,* 1973**

Call me anything, call me *motherfucker*, but don't call me Durocher. A Durocher is the lowest form of living matter.

Harry Wendelstedt, umpire's joke, 1974

If you don't win, you're going to be fired. If you do win, you've only put off the day you're going to be fired.

Leo Durocher, *Nice Guys Finish Last,* 1975

You don't save a pitcher for tomorrow. Tomorrow it may rain.

Leo Durocher

When you cross Durocher you had better be sure that your own jockstrap and cup are in place.

Harold Parrott, *The Lords of Baseball,* 1976

Jim Frey (Kansas City Royals, 1980–81)

If it's true that we learn by our mistakes, then Jim Frey will be the best manager ever.   **Ron Luciano, broadcaster, 1981**

Fred Haney (St. Louis Browns, Pittsburgh Pirates, and Milwaukee Braves, 1939–59)

Fred Haney didn't manage the club. He sat in one corner of the dugout, gulping down pills and saying to Crandall, "What should we do, Del?"

Joey Jay, pitcher, on the 1959 Milwaukee Braves

Fred Hutchinson (Detroit Tigers, St. Louis Cardinals, and Cincinnati Reds, 1952–64)

For five innings, it's the pitcher's game. After that, it's mine.

Fred Hutchinson, 1953

Dark throws stools; Hutch throws rooms.

Ed Bailey, Cincinnati Reds catcher

He always looks like his team has just hit into a game-ending triple play. **Leonard Koppett, *New York Post*, 1959**

There's two things a young ballplayer has to learn early in baseball: Never borrow money from your club and never try to fool your manager.

Fred Hutchinson, Cincinnati Reds manager, 1961

Tom Lasorda (Los Angeles Dodgers, 1976–   )

Cut my veins and Dodger blue will flow. When I die, I want it on my tombstone: "Dodger Stadium was his address, but every ball park was his home." **Tom Lasorda, 1976**

I like the designated-hitter rule because it will cut down on Mr. Lasorda's mistakes.

Don Stanhouse, Los Angeles Dodgers pitcher, 1980

A manager probably makes more decisions in the course of one game than a businessman makes in an entire week.

Tom Lasorda, 1981

You can plant two thousand rows of corn with the fertilizer Lasorda spreads around. **Joe Garagiola, broadcaster, 1981**

I've heard all his old jokes—in three languages.

Steve Garvey, Los Angeles Dodgers infielder, 1982

Bob Lemon (Kansas City Athletics, Chicago White Sox, and New York Yankees, 1970–82)

I don't know what I can tell you; you don't even drink.

**Bob Lemon, when asked for advice
by Chicago White Sox manager Don Kessinger, 1979**

Bob Lemon's face always looks as if it spent the night in a snowbank. **Lowell Cohn,** *San Francisco Chronicle,* **1981**

John McGraw (Baltimore Orioles and New York Giants, 1899–1932)

I think we can win it—if my brains hold out.
> **John McGraw, managing the New York Giants in the frantic 1921 pennant race**

He could take kids out of the coal mines and out of the wheat fields and make them walk and talk and chatter and play ball with the look of eagles.
> **Heywood Broun,** *New York World,* **1924**

His very walk across the field in a hostile town was a challenge to the multitude. **Grantland Rice, sportswriter**

He was the type of fellow who would call all the pitches until you got in a spot, then he'd leave you on your own.
> **Bill Terry, New York Giants infielder, 1928**

Billy Martin (Minnesota Twins, Detroit Tigers, Texas Rangers, New York Yankees, and Oakland A's, 1969–)

Now you take Ernie Lombardi who's a big man and has a big nose and you take Martin who's a little man and has a bigger nose. How do you figger it?
> **Casey Stengel, New York Yankees manager**

When I get through managing, I'm going to open up a kindergarten. **Billy Martin**

Out of twenty-five guys there should be five who would run through a wall for you, two or three who don't like you at all, five who are indifferent and maybe three undecided. My job is to keep the last two groups from going the wrong way.
> **Billy Martin, 1976**

The rules are made by me, but I don't have to follow them.

Billy Martin, 1978

If you approach Billy Martin right, he's O.K. I avoid him altogether.   **Ron Guidry, New York Yankees pitcher, 1978**

A mouse studying to be a rat.

John Schulian, Chicago sportswriter, 1979

He's the kind of guy you'd like to kill if he's playing for the other team, but you'd like ten of him on your side. The little bastard.

Frank Lane, Cleveland Indians general manager, 1979

I had to fight three kids once because I joined the YMCA. They thought I was getting too ritzy for them.

Billy Martin, on his youth in Berkeley, California, 1979

Answer: Yankee go home.
Question: What do bartenders say when Billy Martin shows up?   **Johnny Carson, as "Karnac the Magnificent," 1979**

Martin has established himself as baseball's leading tragedian, a sort of King Lear in double-knits who rants, raves and always dies in the end.   **Diane K. Shah, *Newsweek*, 1980**

The only thing I never learned from Billy Martin was how to knock a guy out in a bar.

**JoAnne Carner, professional golfer,
who says Martin taught her how to win, 1981**

Billy's back . . . May the Lord have mercy on the big guys wherever they are.   **B. J. Phillips, *Time*, 1981**

Billy takes after me. I told my kids, "Don't take nothin' from nobody. If you can't hit 'em, bite 'em."

Joan Downey, Martin's mother, 1981

He made losing absolutely miserable.

Jim Sundberg, Texas Rangers catcher, 1981

Playing for Billy Martin is like being married to him. Right now we're all sleeping on the couch.

Matt Keough, Oakland A's pitcher, 1982

Frank Robinson (Cleveland Indians and San Francisco Giants, 1975–)

I had no trouble communicating. The players just didn't like what I had to say.

Frank Robinson, on managing the Cleveland Indians, 1981

He's really had it rough. He started out as the first black manager, what a burden to carry. And in Cleveland at that. That's where elephants go to die.   **Ron Luciano, former umpire, 1982**

Joe Schultz (Seattle Pilots and Detroit Tigers, 1969–73)

Let's go get 'em and then pound some Budweiser.

Joe Schultz, giving a pep talk to his Seattle Pilots, 1969

Joe's idea of strategy was to come out to the mound, pick up the resin bag, slam it down, and say, "What the shit. Give 'em some low smoke and we'll catch an early plane the hell out of here."   **Jim Bouton, former pitcher, 1973**

Casey Stengel (Brooklyn Dodgers, Boston Braves, New York Yankees, and New York Mets, 1934–65)

I had many years that I was not so successful as a ballplayer, as it is a game of skill.   **Casey Stengel, 1922**

The secret of managing is to keep the guys who hate you away from the guys who are undecided.   **Casey Stengel.**

Every time two owners got together with a fountain pen, Casey Stengel was being sold or bought.

**Quentin Reynolds, writer,
on Stengel's trips around the league as a player**

He can talk all day and all night, on any kind of track, wet or dry. **John Lardner, sportswriter**

The man who has done the most for baseball in Boston this year.
>**Dave Egan, Boston sportswriter,**
>**on the cabdriver who hit Boston Braves manager Stengel**

Everybody knows that Casey Stengel has forgotten more baseball than I'll ever know. That's the trouble, he's forgotten it.
>**Jimmy Piersall, New York Mets outfielder, 1963**

I'm probably the only guy who worked for Stengel before and after he was a genius.
>**Warren Spahn, pitcher, who played**
>**on the Stengel-managed 1942 Boston Braves**
>**and 1965 New York Mets**

It's the first role I've ever played in a foreign language.
>**Charles Durning, actor, portraying Stengel, 1981**

Earl Weaver (Baltimore Orioles, 1968–82)

When I went there, the school was segregated. It's still segregated—except now it's black.
>**Earl Weaver, on his St. Louis high school, 1972**

It's better to lose a game by making a move than lose it sitting on my ass. **Earl Weaver, *Winning!*, 1972**

Love me now, baby, 'cuz on the first of September, I turn into an asshole. **Earl Weaver, 1979**

I could never figure out a way to hate Earl Weaver and still be fair. **Ron Luciano, former umpire, 1980**

The problem with Earl is that he holds a grudge. Hell, he even holds your minor-league record against you.
>**Ron Luciano, 1980**

A manager's job is simple. For 162 games, you try not to screw up all that smart stuff your organization did last December.
Earl Weaver, 1980

It's like you come to a controversy and a ball game breaks out.
Matt Keough, Oakland A's pitcher, on a game between teams managed by Weaver and Billy Martin, 1981

I don't want to win my 300th game while he's still there. He'd take credit for it. **Jim Palmer, Baltimore Orioles pitcher, 1981**

Unfortunately, a player can't throw an umpire out of a game—even though Earl Weaver has tried it a couple of times.
Lon Simmons, San Francisco Giants announcer, 1981

Ted Williams (Washington Senators and Texas Rangers, 1969–72)

All managers are losers; they are the most expendable pieces of furniture on earth.
Ted Williams, just before he became manager of the Washington Senators, 1968

If you don't do any better than last year's last-place finish, people will say it's a lousy team, anyway. If you do better than last year, they'll say you're a hell of a manager.
Bob Short, Washington Senators owner, persuading Williams to become manager, 1969

Some of the players would have hung themselves if I had announced a new five-year contract for Williams.
Bob Short, firing Williams, 1972

Maury Wills (Seattle Mariners, 1981)

Managing is a low-security profession, as I was saying on my way over here to my cab driver, Maury Wills.

Lindsey Nelson, San Francisco Giants announcer,
giving a speech in San Francisco, 1981

Letting him manage in the major leagues is like sending Bo Derek through cellblock A without a bodyguard.

Bill James, *Sport*, 1982

Don Zimmer (San Diego Padres, Boston Red Sox, and Texas Rangers, 1972–82)

I want to make sure nobody is in my uniform.

Don Zimmer, on why he arrives at the park early, 1977

The designated gerbil.   **Bill Lee, Montreal Expos pitcher, 1978**

Zimmer's face looks like a blocked kick.

Joe Garagiola, broadcaster, 1980

Chapter 22

Minor Leagues

I guess I played in more places than sunbeams in a forest. I wound up as the only left-handed shortstop in semipro baseball. **Arthur "Bugs" Baer,** *Collier's,* **1942**

Whoever wants to know the heart and mind of America had better learn baseball, the rules and realities of the game—and do it by watching first some high school or small-town teams.
Jacques Barzun, *God's Country and Mine,* **1954**

When you get hungry enough, you find yourself speaking Spanish pretty well.
Josh Gibson, Negro-leagues catcher, on playing in Cuba

Shucks, those guys couldn't understand the language I was pitching to them in. That's why I struck out so many.
Vinegar Bend Mizell, St. Louis Cardinals pitcher,
playing in the Cuban Winter League, 1951

There are a lot of fellas with all the ability it takes to play in the major leagues, but they never make it, they always get stuck in the minor leagues because they haven't got the guts to make the climb.

Cookie Lavagetto, Washington Senators manager, 1960

Don't worry about a thing. You'll do real fine up on St. Cloud Nine. And if you don't, you just buy the club.

Leon Wagner, San Francisco Giants outfielder, to bonus baby Gaylord Perry, 1961

Little League is the citadel of no-hit, 25–11 games. I think the record number of bases-on-balls was 108 in a doubleheader once. Of course these were second-line pitchers. Front-line pitchers rarely give up over 50 walks a game.

Jim Murray, *The Best of Jim Murray*, 1965

For the parent of a Little Leaguer, a baseball game is simply a nervous breakdown divided into innings.

Earl Wilson, columnist

Wayne, I think you're going to hit .290 this year—but you're going to be doing it in Montgomery, Alabama.

Mayo Smith, Detroit Tigers manager, to Wayne Comer, 1967

I didn't think I was that bad a ballplayer. But they're making a believer out of me.

Jim Gosger, Seattle Pilots outfielder, sent down to Vancouver, 1969

We get used to special privileges and come to expect them. In the minor leagues a baseball player can tear up a bar or impregnate the mayor's daughter and he'll be asked please not let it happen again.   **Jim Bouton, *Ball Four*, 1970**

He's out! Why does he have to run with his blanket?

David Steinberg, comic, to his Little League son, 1971

Come on, Leroy, as long as you've got your thumb in your mouth, throw a spitball.   **Flip Wilson, comic, to his son, 1971**

You know what the Little League is? Something to keep the parents off the street. I bet you don't know what is the first question Little Leaguers always ask me. "How much money do you make?"

Rocky Bridges, Triple-A Hawaii Islanders manager, 1972

It's not a brand-new bus, but it's not an antique. I don't want to put any laurels in my pocket, but it's as good as any bus in the league.

Jack Quinn, Triple-A San Jose Bees president, 1972

I never played on the high school baseball team. To much gee-whiz bullshit and girls jumping up in their skirts with no panties on just to drive you wacky.

Bo Belinsky, former pitcher, 1972

I think it's wonderful. It keeps the kids out of the house.

Yogi Berra, New York Yankees coach, on Little League

Centralia, Illinois, had a field of grass that was never cut. They figured there was no sense wasting a good mower on weeds.

Earl Weaver, *Winning!*, 1972

I'd rather be the shortest player in the majors than the tallest player in the minors.

Fred Patek, Kansas City Royals infielder (five feet, four inches tall), 1973

There are certain preeminent qualifications to managing a minor-league baseball club. You must be white and either a heavy drinker or a cardplayer.   **Howard Cosell, *Cosell*, 1973**

That was real baseball. We weren't playing for the money. We got Mickey Mouse watches that ran backwards.

Bill Lee, Boston Red Sox pitcher, on the College World Series, 1975

I like my players to be married and in debt. That's the way you motivate them.

Ernie Banks, Chicago Cubs minor-league instructor, 1976

A Southern League ground crew consists of one old man with a rake.   **Jim Bouton, former pitcher, 1979**

I think they have bush leagues so that when you come up to the majors you're so happy to be there that the owners can pay you a helluva lot less than you deserve.

Marty Bell, *Breaking Balls*, 1979

This year? I never go untracked. I still can't figure it out. But I guess the Indians did. They sent me to the minors.

Joe Charboneau, Cleveland Indians outfielder, 1981

There's a blind fellow who comes with a friend, and he boos the umps with the rest of the fans.

Miles Wolff, Class-A Durham Bulls owner, 1981

Teaching baseball to five-year-olds is like trying to organize a bunch of earthworms.   **Dorothy C. McConnell, writer, 1981**

Chapter 23

Modern Days/
Olden Days

Whenever I decided to release a guy, I always had his room searched first for a gun. You couldn't take any chances with some of them birds.

Casey Stengel, Brooklyn Dodgers manager, 1935

Old-timers weekends and airplane landings are alike. If you can walk away from them, they're successful.

Casey Stengel, Brooklyn Dodgers manager, 1935

He didn't like morning practice. He said it wasn't in his contract. He tells me, "I only signed for the games."

Frank Oceak, Triple-A Brunswick Pirates manager,
on pitcher Bo Belinsky, 1956

If horses don't eat it, I don't want to play on it.

Richie Allen, Chicago White Sox infielder,
on artificial turf, 1972

Nowadays, they have more trouble packing hair dryers than baseball equipment. **Bob Feller, former pitcher, 1973**

Connie Mack moved players around with his scorecard. Today they use coaches.   **Jim Bouton, former pitcher, 1973**

The fucking times have really changed. I used to carry my fucking bats. Now they carry everything except something that deals with baseball.

Ted Williams, former outfielder,
on attache cases and music machines on road trips, 1973

It's like playing with marbles in a bathtub.

Dave Lemonds, Chicago White Sox pitcher,
on the new artificial turf in Kansas City, 1973

I feel like I know Babe Ruth and Ty Cobb.

Pete Rose, Cincinnati Reds outfielder, 1974

Baseball is the only thing besides the paper clip that hasn't changed.   **Bill Veeck, Chicago White Sox owner, 1974**

In the olden days, the umpire didn't have to take any courses in mind reading. The pitcher *told* you he was going to throw at you.   **Leo Durocher, *Nice Guys Finish Last*, 1975**

I've changed my mind about it. Instead of being bad, it stinks.

Sparky Anderson, Cincinnati Reds manager,
on the designated-hitter rule, 1976

Who voted for the rule? The National League voted unanimously to let the American League use it.

Billy Martin, New York Yankees manager,
on the designated-hitter rule, 1978

Baseball is a country all to itself. It is an old country, like Ruritania, northwest of Bohemia and its seacoast. Steam locomotives puff across trestles and through tunnels. It is a wrong-end-of-the-telescope country, like the landscape people built for model trains, miniature in distance and old age.

Donald Hall, *Baseball, I Gave You*
***All the Best Years of My Life*, 1979**

Baseball is a sport dominated by vital ghosts; it's a fraternity, like no other we have of the active and the no longer so, the living and the dead. **Richard Gilman, "Baseball," 1979**

Kids don't learn the fundamentals of baseball at the games anymore. You should enter a ball park the way you enter a church. **Bill Lee, Montreal Expos pitcher, 1979**

I don't want to go to the National League. I don't want to go through running bases and bunting.
Ed Figueroa, New York Yankees pitcher, 1979

There sure is a lot of bullshit going on in here today. The older you get the better they were when they were younger.
Johnny Sain, pitching coach, 1980

Now more than ever, we need a change of pace in baseball. Ball parks should be happy places. They should always smell like freshly cut grass.
Bill Veeck, Chicago White Sox owner, 1981

Baseball is the most unchanging thing in our society—an island of stability in an unstable world, an island of sanity in an insane world. **Bill Veeck, 1981**

When I think of a stadium, it's like a temple. It's religious. Artificial turf was a desecration. It violated the temple.
Jim Lefebvre, San Francisco Giants coach, 1981

Every day in every way baseball gets fancier and fancier. A few more years and they'll be playing it on Oriental rugs.
Russell Baker, *The New York Times*, 1981

When I started, it was played by nine tough competitors on grass, in graceful ball parks. By the time I was finished, there were ten men on each side, the game was played indoors, on plastic, and I had to spend half my time watching out for a man dressed in a chicken suit who kept trying to kiss me.
Ron Luciano, former umpire, 1982

It is the same game that Moonlight Graham played in 1905. It is a living part of history, like calico dresses, stone crockery, and threshing crews eating at outdoor tables. It continually reminds us of what once was, like an Indian-head penny in a handful of new coins. **W. P. Kinsella,** *Shoeless Joe,* 1982

Every ball park used to be unique. Now it's like women's breasts—if you've seen one, you've seen 'em both.

Jim Kaat, St. Louis Cardinals pitcher, 1982

Chapter 24

Money

This is a funny business. We get paid to knock the cover off the ball, and pitchers get paid to keep us from hitting it.

Bug Holliday, Cincinnati Reds outfielder

I won't play for a penny less than *fifteen hundred* dollars.

Honus Wagner, Pittsburgh Pirates infielder,
rejecting an offer of $2000

It is a strange fact that the highest-salaried teams sometimes come nearest to setting new records for total defeats. That a club wins a pennant or finishes second is no sign that it is well paid. **Ring Lardner, "The Cost of Baseball," 1912**

With the salary I get here, I'm so hollow and starving that I'm liable to explode like a light bulb if I hit the ground too hard.

Casey Stengel, Pittsburgh Pirates outfielder,
explaining to his manager why he didn't slide, 1918

Every time we had a payday we had to sell a ballplayer.
Fresco Thompson, former infielder,
on the 1920s Philadelphia Phillies

I had a better year than he did.
Babe Ruth, New York Yankees outfielder,
when told that his offered salary was more
than President Herbert C. Hoover's, 1930

Give me what I want and I'll take care of myself.
Marty Marion, St. Louis Cardinals infielder,
when told by Branch Rickey, "Accept terms
I have offered and I'll take care of you," 1941

If I was being paid $30,000 a year, the very least I could do
was hit .400.
Ted Williams, former outfielder, on hitting .406 in 1941

I got a million dollars' worth of free advice and a very small
raise.
Eddie Stanky, Brooklyn Dodgers infielder,
after negotiations with Branch Rickey, 1945

Money and women. They're the two strongest things in the
world. The things you do for a woman you wouldn't do for
anything else. Same with money.
Satchel Paige, St. Louis Browns pitcher,
when asked why he kept playing, 1953

Jeez. They're going to give me fifty thousand smackers just
for *living*.
Dizzy Dean, former pitcher,
when he optioned the film rights to his life, 1951

Me take out insurance! Why, for goodness' sakes, if anything
ever happened to me, my mother and father would kill themselves.
Billy Loes, Brooklyn Dodgers pitcher, after signing
a big contract and being advised to take out insurance, 1952

I wouldn't pay that much to a *first* baseman.
                    Samuel Goldwyn, film executive,
                    on a high salary paid to a third baseman

I wish I could buy you for what you're really worth, and sell you for what you think you're worth.
                    Mickey Mantle, New York Yankees outfielder,
                    to teammate Joe Pepitone

I look at the ball, and I see dollar signs instead of stitches.
                    Carl Furillo, Los Angeles Dodgers outfielder, 1959

Beer makes some people happy. Winning ball games makes some people happy. Cashing checks makes me delirious with joy. **Jim Brosnan, Cincinnati Reds pitcher, 1961**

A ballplayer's got to be kept hungry to become a big-leaguer. That's why no boy from a rich family ever made the big leagues. **Joe DiMaggio, former outfielder, 1961**

It's kind of discouraging to realize I'm the lowest-paid member of the Yale class of 'fifty-six.
                    Ken MacKenzie, New York Mets pitcher, 1962

I went back to Philly to talk contract with Mr. Nugent. My hotel and food cost me more while I was there negotiating than the raise I got. **Kirby Higbe, *The High Hard One*, 1967**

I'm sure we'll be able to work out a fair price for your services, based on the fact that you are unemployed.
                    Marvin Kitman, comic writer,
                    claiming Dick Stuart for the $1 waiver price, 1968

Don't be afraid to climb those golden stairs. Go in there and get what you're worth.
                    Johnny Sain, Seattle Pilots coach,
                    advising Jim Bouton on salary demands, 1969

You don't need a lawyer to tell the club you had a lousy year.
Bill Stoneman, Montreal Expos pitcher,
on why he didn't use an agent to negotiate his contract, 1971

I was a bonus baby. I got two autographed baseballs and a scorecard from the 1935 All-Star Game.
Bob Feller, former pitcher, on his 1936 rookie contract, 1972

I'm the most loyal player money can buy.
Don Sutton, Los Angeles Dodgers pitcher, 1975

I don't need a raise. I'm still in the game. That's what counts.
Mark Fidrych, Detroit Tigers pitcher,
making the minimum salary as a rookie, 1976

You're making too much at a young age. It isn't good for you.
M. Donald Grant, New York Mets chairman,
rejecting Tom Seaver's pay demands, 1977

Life is a game, but the way to keep score is money.
Ted Turner, Atlanta Braves owner, 1978

With the money I'm making, I should be playing two positions.   **Pete Rose, Philadelphia Phillies infielder, 1979**

We will scheme, connive and steal and do everything possible to win a pennant—everything except pay big salaries.
Bill Veeck, Chicago White Sox owner, 1979

I play the game in my mind. I see the hitters in my mind and figure out how to get them out. I tried to play out my contract problem that way, too, but it didn't work out.
Craig Swan, New York Mets pitcher, 1979

When we played, World Series' checks meant something. Now all they do is screw up your taxes.
Don Drysdale, California Angels announcer, 1980

These guys are so rich I'm surprised they don't play the game on horseback. And in pith helmets. It's got to be easy to strike out a guy worried about the federal re-discount rate.

Jim Murray, *Los Angeles Times*, 1980

You measure the value of a ballplayer on how many fannies he puts in the seats.

George Steinbrenner, New York Yankees owner, 1980

I coined the phrase Lords of Baseball when owners were absolute. Now, we have millionaires masquerading as proletariat, the Limousine Laborers.

Dick Young, New York *Daily News*, 1981

It's changed so much. They sign for bonuses. If you know where home plate is: $50,000. If you know where first base is: $25,000. Joe Garagiola, broadcaster, 1981

I'm a top entertainer in my field. And those guys, like the bank president, in their own way are important also.

Andre Dawson, Montreal Expos outfielder,
explaining why he makes $300,000 a year more
than the Bank of America president, 1981

Baseball players ought to try playing golf for a living. No guarantees, all expense paid—by yourself. I'd like to hear them complain then. Al Geiberger, professional golfer, 1981

On the scoreboard are the Dow-Jones averages. We can remember when the bible of baseball was *The Sporting News,* not the *Wall Street Journal.* For those of you scoring at home: thirty-two million shares were traded today. Utility players: one closed down 107.53.

Hank Greenwald, San Francisco Giants announcer, 1981

I don't mind the high price of stardom. I just don't like the high price of mediocrity.

Bill Veeck, Chicago White Sox owner, 1981

Chapter 25

Outfielders

Henry Aaron (1954–76)

Henry Aaron is the only ballplayer I have ever seen who goes to sleep at the plate. But trying to sneak a fastball past him is like trying to sneak the sunrise past a rooster.

Curt Simmons, Philadelphia Phillies pitcher

It wasn't a bad pitch, but it wasn't good enough against Hank Aaron.

Jack Billingham, Cincinnati Reds pitcher,
on giving up Aaron's 714th home run, 1974

I'm mad at Hank for deciding to play one more season. I threw him his last home run and thought I'd be remembered forever. Now I'll have to throw him another.

Bill Lee, Boston Red Sox pitcher, 1976

Cool Papa Bell (Negro leagues, 1922–46)

Cool Papa Bell was so fast he could get out of bed, turn out the lights across the room and be back in bed under the covers before the lights went out.

Josh Gibson, Negro-leagues catcher

One hit he hit a line drive right past my ear. I turned around and saw the ball hit his ass sliding into second.

Satchel Paige, Negro-leagues pitcher

They used to say, "If we find a *good* black player, we'll sign him." They was lying.   **Cool Papa Bell**

French Bordagary (1934–45)

He's either the greatest rotten third baseman in baseball or the rottenest great third baseman. But he's never in between.

Branch Rickey, St. Louis Cardinals general manager, 1938

Lou Brock (1961–79)

I guess I'd better send my fingers to Cooperstown.

Dennis Lamp, Chicago Cubs pitcher, after Brock got his three-thousandth hit off Lamp's pitching hand, 1979

Ty Cobb (1905–28)

His trouble is he takes life too seriously. Cobb is going at it too hard.   **Cy Young, Boston Braves pitcher**

The Babe was a great ballplayer, sure. But Cobb was even greater. Babe could knock your brains out, but Cobb would drive you crazy.   **Tris Speaker, outfielder**

To him, a ballgame wasn't a mere athletic contest. It was a knock-'em-down, crush 'em, relentless war. He was their enemy, and if they got in his way he ran right over them.

Moe Berg, catcher

That's easy. You just take a gun and shoot him.

Ring Lardner, on how to get Cobb out

He was gamer than a dentist pulling his own teeth and could take it like a carpet on the line. But he was as touchy as finger-print powder and would climb a mountain to take a punch at an echo.   **Arthur "Bugs" Baer, *Collier's*, 1942**

He did everything—except steal first base. And I think he did that in the dead of night.

Rube Bressler, former outfielder, 1966

Willie Davis (1960–76)

That Davis is so fast his head's three feet behind the rest of him.   **Jocko Conlan, umpire, 1961**

He can run, hit, throw and field. The only thing Willie Davis has never been able to do is think.

Buzzie Bavasi, California Angels general manager, 1979

Joe DiMaggio (1936–51)

It proves that no man can be a success in two national pas-times.

**Oscar Levant, pianist,
on DiMaggio's divorce from Marilyn Monroe, 1955**

Joe is a man who was meant to play ball on hot afternoons on the grass of big cities. He never belonged in the rain.

Jimmy Cannon, *Sport*, 1956

Would he hit safely in every game forever? It seemed that way. And why not? He was only 26 and playing baseball in the sunshine. He heard little boys cheer, not cry.

Raymond Chandler, *Farewell, My Lovely*, 1940

I want to thank my teammates who scored so many runs and Joe DiMaggio, who ran down my mistakes.

**Lefty Gomez, former pitcher,
at Gomez' Hall of Fame induction, 1972**

Joe DiMaggio batting sometimes gave the impression—the suggestion that the old rules and dimensions of baseball no longer applied to him, and that the game had at last grown unfairly easy.   **Roger Angell,** *The Summer Game,* **1972**

Mike Epstein (1966–74)

Unfortunately, we couldn't get the Pasadena space people on it because they were busy with some Apollo mission or something.

**Rocky Bridges, manager,
on an Epstein tape-measure home run, 1967**

He simply does not know his own strength. The way he makes peace, a man would prefer war.

Myron Cope, *Broken Cigars,* **1968**

George Foster (1969–   )

You're gonna hit 50 homers and drive in 140 runs living a clean life. Why don't you just hit 40 and get 125 RBIs and mess around a little?

Joe Morgan, Cincinnati Reds infielder, 1977

Your basic George Foster home run. It probably would have killed four people and broken three seats.

Ed Ott, Pittsburgh Pirates catcher, 1979

If you prefer baseball action in slow motion, don't miss George Foster chasing a double into the left-field corner.

Charles Bricker, *San Jose Mercury,* **1981**

You have to get your uniform dirty. I used to use three uniforms every day. George uses three a month.
> **Pete Rose, Philadelphia Phillies infielder, 1982**

I slide when I have to slide. But I'm going to be trotting around the bases a lot more than Pete will be trotting.
> **George Foster, to Rose, 1982**

Oscar Gamble (1969–   )

Oscar Gamble hits as if he were worth his $450,000 salary—but plays the field as if he were carrying the full bulging amount in his uniform.   **Pete Axthelm, *Inside Sports*, 1979**

Oscar is so old that when he broke into the majors he was still a Negro.   **Stan Williams, New York Yankees coach, 1981**

Babe Herman (1926–45)

He did not always catch fly balls on the top of his head, but he could do it in a pinch. He never tripled into a triple play, but he once doubled into a double play, which is the next best thing.   **John Lardner, sportswriter**

He wore a glove for only one reason: it was a league custom. The glove would last him a minimum of six years because it rarely made contact with the ball.
> **Fresco Thompson, *Every Diamond Doesn't Sparkle*, 1964**

Frank Howard (1958–73)

One of these days Howard will unleash a line drive at the opposing pitcher and the only identification left on the mound is going to be a laundry mark.
> **Fresco Thompson, *Every Diamond Doesn't Sparkle*, 1964**

Clomping around in the outfield, he catches hell from the crowds more than he catches anything else.
> **Ron Smith, *True*, 1969**

He swings and swings and swings. Someday a pitcher with a good move is going to throw over to first base. . . . and Frank Howard will swing at it.

Pete Reiser, Los Angeles Dodgers coach, 1969

The guy ain't human. Every time he comes to the plate I keep looking behind to see where it is you wind it up.

Duke Sims, Cleveland Indians catcher, 1969

Reggie Jackson (1967–   )

There isn't enough mustard in the whole world to cover that hot dog. **Darold Knowles, Oakland A's pitcher, 1974**

He'd give you the shirt off his back. Of course, he'd call a press conference to announce it.

Catfish Hunter, New York Yankees pitcher, 1977

I couldn't quit . . . because of all the kids and the blacks and the little people who are pulling for me. I represent both the underdog *and* the overdog in our society.

Reggie Jackson, 1977

Your first name's white, your second is Hispanic and your third belongs to a black. No wonder you don't know who you are.

Mickey Rivers, New York Yankees outfielder, 1977

Off the record, he's a piece of shit.

Billy Martin, New York Yankees manager, 1977

It's not that Reggie is a bad outfielder. He just has trouble judging the ball and picking it up. **Billy Martin, 1978**

When you unwrap a Reggie bar, it tells you how good it is.

Catfish Hunter, New York Yankees pitcher, 1978

I go back to 1965 with Reggie, but I guess I don't go far enough back to remember when he was shy.

Rick Monday, Los Angeles Dodgers outfielder, 1980

Reggie always believes he has the upper hand. He thinks pitchers are moaning, "Oh, no, here comes Reggie Jackson."

Fran Healy, New York Yankees broadcaster, 1980

Just as nature fills a vacuum, Reggie fills a spotlight.

Bob Marshall, *Diary of a Yankee-Hater*, 1981

Mark Twain said that politicians, old buildings, and prostitutes become respectable with age. Reggie Jackson would like to make it a foursome.

Thomas Boswell, *How Life Imitates the World Series*, 1982

Alex Johnson (1964–76)

I saw him play a game completely in the shade one day. He just didn't want to play in the sun.   **Ron Luciano, umpire, 1980**

Jay Johnstone (1966–   )

What makes him unusual is that he thinks he's normal and everyone else is nuts.

Danny Ozark, Philadelphia Phillies manager, 1975

Dave Kingman (1971–   )

Kingman, about whose personality we can say absolutely nothing.   **Dick Schaap, "PBS Latenight," PBS-TV, 1982**

Garry Maddox (1972–   )

Two-thirds of the earth is covered by water, the other one-third is covered by Garry Maddox.

Ralph Kiner, Pittsburgh Pirates announcer, 1973

He's turned his life around. He used to be depressed and miserable. Now he's miserable and depressed.

Harry Kalas, Philadelphia Phillies announcer, 1981

Mickey Mantle (1951–68)

When Mickey Mantle's playing first base he imitates Stan Musial. Everybody else is imitating Mickey Mantle and Mickey Mantle's imitating Stan Musial.

Casey Stengel, New York Yankees manager

Mantle ran into the training room after a bad day like a rat running back into his hole.

Dick Young, New York *Daily News*

Mantle's idea of keeping fit was to have an active social life and play golf out of an electric cart which was outfitted with a bar.   **Leonard Shecter, *The Jocks*, 1970**

The body of a god. Only Mantle's legs are mortal.

Jerry Coleman, former infielder, 1971

Everybody who roomed with Mickey said he took five years off their career.   **Whitey Ford, former pitcher, 1977**

Mickey loves people, he always overtips, and he's big-hearted. He's got a heart as big as Yankee Stadium.

Billy Martin, *Number 1*, 1980

Roger Maris (1951–68)

That Maris. You'd tell him something and he'd stare at you for a week before answering.

Casey Stengel, New York Yankees manager

Look at this. My goddamn hair is coming out. Did your hair ever fall out from playing baseball?

**Roger Maris,
feeling the pressure of going for sixty-one home runs, 1961**

It would be a shame if Ruth's record is broken by a .270 hitter.

Rogers Hornsby, former infielder, 1961

Willie Mays (1951–73)

The ball came down in Utica. I know. I was managing there
at the time.
                    Lefty Gomez, on Mays' first career home run, 1951

Joe Louis, Jascha Heifetz, Sammy Davis, and Nashua rolled
into one.   **Leo Durocher, New York Giants manager, 1955**

Harvey Kuenn gave it an honest pursuit, but the only center
fielder in baseball who could have caught it hit it.
                    Bob Stevens, on Mays' game-winning triple
            in the All-Star Game, *San Francisco Chronicle*, 1959

Look at him. *He* knows he's going to hit me, and *I* know he's
going to hit, so I'm going to walk him.
                    Harvey Haddix, Pittsburgh Pirates pitcher,
                                        to his catcher, 1961

As the ball left the bat, I said to myself two things. The first
thing I said was, "Hello, double!" The second thing I said
was, "Oh, shit, *he's* out there."
                    Clete Boyer, New York Yankees infielder,
                    on a ball he hit in the World Series, 1962

The secret weapon . . . is the frivolity in his bloodstream. . . .
Willie Mays has doubled his strength with laughter.
                    Branch Rickey, *The American Diamond*, 1965

Mays threw so many baserunners out he may lead the entire
Giant infield in assists. He should play in handcuffs to even
things up a bit.   **Jim Murray, *Los Angeles Times*, 1966**

I can't very well tell my batters don't hit it to him. Wherever
they hit it, he's there anyway.
                    Gil Hodges, New York Mets manager, 1969

You used to think if the score was 5–0, he'd hit a five-run
homer.   **Reggie Jackson, Oakland A's outfielder, 1973**

Such golden creatures—a young Willie Mays, say—are awesome to observe but not especially rewarding as a subject for study: one can take apart a pocket watch but not a sunset.

Roger Angell, *Late Innings*, 1982

Joe Medwick (1932–48)

Dawgonnit, that Medwick don't fight fair at all. You argue with him for a bit and then he beats you before you've even had a chance to speak your piece.

Dizzy Dean, St. Louis Cardinals pitcher

That Medwick never lost a debate in his life, mostly because he didn't bother. He was a one-man rampage.

Leo Durocher, *Nice Guys Finish Last*, 1975

Bobby Murcer (1965–)

Murcer's job is to sit on the bench and personify the Yankees' awesome depth. Bob Marshall, *Diary of a Yankee-Hater*, 1981

Stan Musial (1941–63)

Musial's batting stance looks like a small boy looking around a corner to see if the cops are coming.

Ted Lyons, Chicago White Sox pitcher, 1941

I've had pretty good success with Stan. By throwing him my best pitch and backing up third.

Carl Erskine, Brooklyn Dodgers pitcher

You guys are trying to stop Musial in fifteen minutes when the National ain't stopped him in fifteen years.

Yogi Berra,
going over the hitters before the All-Star Game, 1956

Once Musial timed your fastball, your infielders were in jeopardy.   **Warren Spahn, Milwaukee Braves pitcher, 1964**

It's ridiculous that we are gathered here tonight to honor a man who made more than 7,000 outs.
**Bob Prince, Pittsburgh Pirates announcer,
at Musial's retirement dinner, 1964**

He could have hit .300 with a fountain pen.
Joe Garagiola, broadcaster, 1981

Jimmy Piersall (1950–67)

He showed them it was a game, so they locked him up.
Abbie Hoffman, writer and former Yippie, 1977

Lou Piniella (1964–   )

Goddamn, he catches every ball he can get to. He's the best slow outfielder in baseball.   **Sparky Lyle, *The Bronx Zoo*, 1979**

"Sweet" refers to Lou's swing, not his personality.
Phil Rizzuto, New York Yankees announcer, 1981

Rick Reichardt (1964–74)

The first time I saw him, I thought he fell out of a Wheaties box.   **Joe Garagiola, broadcaster, 1964**

His only weakness is he's gotta shave twice a day.
Chuck Tanner, minor-league manager, 1964

Dusty Rhodes (1952–59)

Any time you see a fielder get under a ball and pound his glove—even in Little League—you know he's going to catch it. I have seen Rhodes pound his glove and have the ball fall twenty feet behind him.
Leo Durocher, *Nice Guys Finish Last*, 1975

Jim Rice (1974–   )

I swallowed my tobacco both times.

> Don Zimmer, Boston Red Sox manager,
> on two five-hundred-foot homers by Rice, 1978

I've never heard a bat louder than his. You hear it going through the strike zone and the sound is unmistakable. It goes *Vump*. That's when he misses.

> Ken Harrelson, Boston Red Sox announcer, 1980

Frank Robinson (1956–76)

Going over the hitters it was decided that we should pitch Frank Robinson underground.   Jim Bouton, *Ball Four*, 1970

He can step on your shoes, but he doesn't mess up your shine.

> Joe Morgan, San Francisco Giants infielder,
> on Robinson's tact as a manager, 1981

Babe Ruth (1914–35)

The more I see of Babe, the more he seems a figure out of mythology.   Burt Whitman, Boston sportswriter, 1918

I don't room with him. I room with his suitcase.

> Ping Bodie, New York Yankees outfielder,
> on an exhibition tour with Ruth, 1920

How that man loved to eat. If he'd ever been sawed in half on any given day, I think three-fourths of Stevens' concessions would have been found inside him.   Ty Cobb

He would not have known how to deal with an enemy for the simple reason that he never had one.

> Frank Graham, *Sport*, 1954

He was the most uninhibited human being I have ever known. He just did things.   John Drebinger, *The New York Times*

To try to capture Ruth with cold statistics would be like trying to keep up with him on a night out.

Bob Broeg, *The Sporting News*

He was a parade all by himself, a burst of dazzle and jingle,
Santa Claus drinking his whiskey straight.

Jimmy Cannon, sportswriter

The only sports legend I ever saw who completely lived up
to advance billing was Babe Ruth.

Jimmy Breslin, *Can't Anybody Here Play This Game?*, 1963

He was a damn animal. He had that instinct. They know when
it's going to rain, things like that. Nature—that was Ruth!

Rube Bressler, former pitcher, 1965

I always figured the best way to pitch to Ruth, especially in a
pinch, was to walk him. Maybe that's why I stayed in the
league so long.   **Sam Jones, former pitcher, 1965**

As he moved, center stage moved with him.

Roger Kahn, *How the Weather Was*, 1973

Some twenty years ago, I stopped talking about the Babe for
the simple reason that I realized that those who had never
seen him didn't believe me.

Tommy Holmes, sportswriter, 1975

Every big-league player and his wife should teach their children to pray: "God bless mommy, God bless daddy, and God
bless Babe Ruth."

**Waite Hoyt, former pitcher,
on Ruth bringing in the fans and big salaries, 1977**

Babe Ruth ate and he slept around and he played baseball.
Those were the three things he did in life.

Herb Michelson, former sportswriter, 1981

I tell my pitchers to throw strikes. There has only been one Babe Ruth and he's been dead for thirty years.

Art Fowler, Oakland A's pitching coach, 1981

Ron Swoboda (1965–73)

He's the kind of kid who will turn around quickly in a bus and catch you in the eye with an elbow. Somebody's in danger every time he moves.

Ernie White, minor-league manager, 1964

Gorman Thomas (1973–   )

He received fourteen letters when he was in high school. I earned one, but it was from the principal.

Lon Simmons, Oakland A's announcer, 1981

Paul Waner (1926–45)

Paul Waner was always sipping from a Coke bottle in the dugout. One day, while he was batting, a new batboy snuck a long swig. The kid woke up with a crashing hangover.

Mike Royko, *Chicago Sun-Times*, 1981

Claudell Washington (1974–   )

He plays the outfield like he's trying to catch grenades.

Reggie Jackson, New York Yankees outfielder, 1977

Ted Williams (1939–60)

My name is Ted fucking Williams and I'm the greatest hitter in baseball.

Ted Williams, psyching himself up in the batting cage

We have three big leagues now. There's the American, the National, and there's Ted Williams.

Mickey Harris, Boston Red Sox pitcher, 1946

By the time the press of Boston has completed its daily treatment of Theodore S. Williams, there is no room in the papers for anything but two sticks of agate type about Truman and housing, and one column for the last Boston girl to be murdered on a beach.   **John Lardner, sportswriter**

Yeah, you can pitch him low, but as soon as you throw the ball run and hide behind second base.

Lou Boudreau, Cleveland Indians manager

If he'd just tip his cap once, he could be elected mayor of Boston in five minutes.   **Eddie Collins, former infielder, 1962**

I got a big charge out of *seeing* Ted Williams hit. Once in a while they let me try to field some of them, which sort of dimmed my enthusiasm.

Rocky Bridges, former infielder, 1972

Hack Wilson (1923–34)

Hack Wilson usually played in the outfield, but I'd put him at first base because he wouldn't have as far to stagger to the dugout.   **Mike Royko, *Chicago Sun-Times*, 1981**

He jumped into the stands and beat up a fan. He later said he wasn't really mad at the fan, but he wanted to get arrested so he could take his hangover out of the hot sun.

Bill Veeck, Chicago White Sox owner, 1981

Carl Yastrzemski (1961–   )

Most Valuable Player from the neck down.

Eddie Stanky, Chicago White Sox manager, 1967

Baseball tests your emotional stability. You have to be emotionally identical every day. Oh, no, I'm not talking about myself. I'm thinking of Carl Yastrzemski.

Carlton Fisk, Boston Red Sox catcher, 1980

Just when it seems Yaz is to become a living museum piece, he surges back. **George Vescey, *The New York Times*, 1982**

Chapter 26

Owners and
Executives

A fellow bossing a big league ball club is busier than a one-armed paperhanger with the flying hives.
Ty Cobb, *Bustin' Em and Other Big League Stories,* 1914

If Joe Stallion knowed how much money there was in the concessions at a ball park, he'd get outta politics and get in an honest business. **Dizzy Dean, former pitcher**

Bobo Newsom claims we had a gentlemen's agreement on his contract. Couldn't be. No gentlemen were involved.
Joe Engel, Triple-A Chattanooga Lookouts president

The commissioner is a czar with absolute powers over anything that doesn't concern baseball.
Jimmy Cannon, sportswriter, 1957

The last people who went broke in baseball were Roy and Earl Mack, Connie's sons. And I claim they did it on merit.
Red Smith, on the Philadelphia Athletics owners,
The New York Times

Connie Mack's sons became senile before Connie did.

Jimmy Isaminger, *Philadelphia Inquirer*

We live by the Golden Rule. Those who have the gold make the rules. **Buzzie Bavasi, Brooklyn Dodgers general manager**

I have a darn good job with the Cardinals, but please don't ask me what I do.

Stan Musial, on his front-office job with St. Louis, 1964

Jeez. They went and got the unknown soldier.

**Larry Fox, sportswriter,
when William Eckert was chosen as commissioner, 1965**

A baseball club is part of the chemistry of the city. A game isn't just an athletic contest. It's a picnic, a kind of town meeting. **Michael Burke, New York Yankees president, 1971**

Bob Short should be named Minor League Executive of the Year.

**Russ White, sportswriter,
on the Texas Rangers owner, 1972**

Is baseball a business? If it isn't, General Motors is a sport.

Jim Murray, *Los Angeles Times*

All I ever wanted to be president of was the American League.

A. Bartlett Giamatti, president of Yale University, 1978

If you dust off old junk sometimes you come up with a gem.

**Bill Veeck, Chicago White Sox owner,
taking a chance on an older player, 1978**

I signed Oscar Gamble on the advice of my attorney. I no longer have Gamble and I no longer have my attorney.

Ray Kroc, San Diego Padres owner, 1979

The baseball mind is a jewel in the strict sense—that is to say, a stone of special value, rare beauty, and extreme hardness. Cut, polished and fixed in the Tiffany setting of a club owner's skull, it resists change as a diamond resists erosion.

Red Smith, *The New York Times*

In the building I live in on Park Avenue, there are ten people who could buy the Yankees, but none of them could hit the ball out of Yankee Stadium.

Reggie Jackson, New York Yankees outfielder, 1981

Front-office brilliance is rarer in baseball than the triple play.

Roger Angell, *Late Innings*, 1982

The National League owners are locked in cement on many ideas. I think it was a long time before any of them had inside plumbing.

Edward Bennett Williams, Baltimore Orioles owner, 1982

Charles O. Finley (Owner, Kansas City Athletics, and Oakland Athletics, 1960–80)

Oakland is the luckiest city since Hiroshima.

Stuart Symington, Missouri senator, when Finley moved his franchise from Kansas City to Oakland, 1967

Mr. Finley pointed out I only used one arm.

Vida Blue, Oakland A's pitcher, on why he wasn't paid more, 1971

Twenty-two out of the twenty-five guys on our team hate him.

Sal Bando, Oakland A's infielder, 1974

Being around him made me feel well.

Jimmy Piersall, former outfielder and mental patient, 1975

Finley is a self-made man who worships his creator.

Jim Murray, *Los Angeles Times*, 1979

Charlie Finley hiring Billy Martin is like Captain Hook hiring the alligator.

Johnny Carson, "The Tonight Show," NBC-TV, 1980

He'd want to know why there were fourteen uniforms dirty when only ten men got in the game.

Frank Ciensczk, Oakland equipment manager, 1981

It took 8 hours, 7½ just to find his heart.

**Steve McCatty, Oakland A's pitcher,
on Finley's heart operation, 1981**

Ford Frick (Commissioner, 1951–65)

Let that be lesson number one on your new job. Never go looking for trouble. Let 'em come to you.

**Judge Landis, commissioner,
to his replacement, Frick, 1951**

I don't know how he ever found his way around New York. If you let him out of his office, he would never find his way back. **Bo Belinsky, California Angels pitcher**

Bowie Kuhn (Commissioner, 1969–)

Bowie is the best commissioner in baseball today.

Jim Bouton, former pitcher, 1978

He says I tamper with the game, but he's the one tampering and always trying to speed it up. Baseball is good enough to sell itself. You don't see a lot of ads for Hershey Bars, do you? **Bill Lee, Montreal Expos pitcher, 1981**

I have often called Bowie Kuhn a village idiot. I apologize to the village idiots of America. He is the nation's idiot.

Charles O. Finley, former Oakland A's owner, 1981

If I hear Bowie Kuhn say just once more he's doing something for the betterment of baseball, I'm going to throw up.

Sparky Anderson, Detroit Tigers manager, 1981

Larry MacPhail (President, Cincinnati Reds, Brooklyn Dodgers, and New York Yankees, 1933–48)

There is a thin line between genius and insanity, and in Larry's case it was sometimes so thin you could see him drifting back and forth.

Leo Durocher, *Nice Guys Finish Last*, 1975

Durocher claims he was sacked forty times [by MacPhail] in his five years as Dodger manager; but I was there, and I can verify only twenty-seven.

Harold Parrott, *The Lords of Baseball*, 1976

The Redhead is so careful of the truth, he uses it very sparingly.   **Dan Parker, sportswriter**

Branch Rickey (Executive and Manager, St. Louis Browns, St. Louis Cardinals, Pittsburgh Pirates, and Brooklyn Dodgers, 1913–49)

A man opposed to Sunday baseball except when the gate receipts exceeded $5,000.   **John Lardner, sportswriter**

It was easy to figure out Mr. Rickey's thinking about contracts. He had both players *and* money—and just didn't like to see the two of them mix.   **Chuck Connors, former infielder**

The only way I know is through God, and Mr. Rickey may not want to speak with him.

Buzzie Bavasi, Brooklyn Dodgers general manager, when Mrs. Rickey wanted to contact Rickey

He didn't like to pay out money. He'd go into the vault to get you a nickel change.   **Enos Slaughter, former infielder, 1975**

George Steinbrenner (Owner, New York Yankees, 1973–   )

As soon as I apologized, I knew he'd spend the rest of the season getting my ass.

Billy Martin, New York Yankees manager,
after Steinbrenner chewed him out, 1977

The more we lose, the more Steinbrenner will fly in. And the more he flies, the better the chance there will be a plane crash.

Graig Nettles, New York Yankees infielder,
at spring training, 1977

I hope to have Steinbrenner ousted as American League president this winter and get somebody other than him running the league.   **Earl Weaver, Baltimore Orioles manager, 1980**

Owning the Yankees is like owning the Mona Lisa; it's something that you'd never sell.   **George Steinbrenner, 1981**

It was a beautiful thing to behold, with all thirty-six oars working in unison.

Jack Buck, St. Louis Cardinals announcer,
on Steinbrenner's new yacht, 1981

Some teams are under the gun; we're under the thumb. The sweetest words to George are "Yes, boss."

Graig Nettles, New York Yankees infielder, 1981

He really should stick to horses. At least he can shoot them if they spit the bit.

Reggie Jackson, California Angels outfielder, 1982

I tell George what I think and then I do what he says.

Bob Lemon, New York Yankees manager, 1982

George Steinbrenner talks out of both sides of his wallet.

Ron Luciano, former umpire, 1982

Give me a bastard with talent.

Saying on a pillow in George Steinbrenner's office, 1982

Seeing as how none of us have ever worked for Genghis Khan, how does it feel to work for George Steinbrenner?

**Ted Dawson, Los Angeles broadcaster,
interviewing manager Gene Michael, 1982**

Ted Turner (Owner, Atlanta Braves, 1976–   )

There's a fine line between being colorful and being an asshole, and I hope I'm still just colorful.　**Ted Turner, 1978**

The man has mistaken his larynx for a megaphone.

Steven Reddicliffe, writer, 1981

Chapter 27

Philosophy

I've got a new invention. It's a revolving bowl for tired gold-fish.   **Lefty Gomez, New York Yankees pitcher, 1930**

I'd rather be lucky than good.
**Lefty Gomez, after a win in which
all the outs were made by his fielders**

It ain't braggin' if you can back it up.
Dizzy Dean, St. Louis Cardinals pitcher

Luck is the residue of design.
Branch Rickey, St. Louis Cardinals general manager

If you tell a lie, always rehearse it. If it don't sound good to you, it won't sound good to anybody.
Satchel Paige, Cleveland Indians pitcher

Ability: the art of getting credit for all the home runs somebody else hits.   **Casey Stengel, New York Yankees manager**

The trick is growing up without growing old.

Casey Stengel

Most people are dead at my age, anyway. You could look it up.

Casey Stengel

The game isn't over till it's over.

Yogi Berra, New York Yankees catcher

If you want to see the sun shine you have to weather the storm.

Frank Lane, Kansas City Athletics general manager, 1961

Sweat plus sacrifice equals success.

Charles O. Finley, Kansas City Athletics owner

It's what you learn after you know it all that counts.

Earl Weaver, Baltimore Orioles manager, 1968

It doesn't hurt to say you're sorry, even if you don't mean it.

Mike Marshall, Seattle Pilots pitcher, 1969

Life is like baseball and we all go through slumps.

Mike Epstein, Oakland A's infielder, to Curt Flood, 1970

Show me a guy who's afraid to look bad, and I'll show you a guy you can beat every time.

Lou Brock, St. Louis Cardinals outfielder

Luck's a hell of a thing. If you've got it, you can make bad moves and still come out good.

Bob Short, Texas Rangers owner, on how he amassed his fortune, 1972

You know when you got it made? When you get your name in the crossword puzzles.

Rocky Bridges, Triple-A Phoenix Giants manager, 1973

An hour after the game, you want to go out and play them again. **Rocky Bridges, on playing the Japanese, 1974**

Do for yourself or do without.
Gaylord Perry, Cleveland Indians pitcher, 1974

You've got to be very careful if you don't know where you are going, because you might not get there.
Yogi Berra, New York Yankees coach, 1974

I think anything you try to do to change anything, even if you explain it to them, the majority of people object.
Philip K. Wrigley, Chicago Cubs owner

When you don't look like you're going to make it, nobody tries to help. When it looks like you're going to be a big-leaguer, everybody has advice, hoping for some credit.
Johnny Sain, pitching coach

A religious fanatic is somebody who knows Jesus Christ better than you do.   **Jim Kaat, Chicago White Sox pitcher, 1975**

Booze, broads, and bullshit. If you got all that, what else do you need?   **Harry Caray, Chicago White Sox announcer, 1976**

Sometime I get lazy and let the dishes stack up. But they don't stack too high. I've only got four dishes.
Mark Fidrych, Detroit Tigers pitcher, 1976

If what you did yesterday still looks big to you, you haven't done much today.
Wid Matthews, Chicago Cubs general manager

Money talks, bullshit walks.
Charles O. Finley, Oakland A's owner

The sun don't shine on the same dog's ass all the time.
**Catfish Hunter, New York Yankees pitcher,
after losing a game in the World Series, 1977**

Babe Ruth struck out 1330 times.
Graffito, New York City, 1977

Life is not important except in the impact it has on other lives.   **Jackie Robinson, former infielder, 1977**

You can have money piled to the ceiling, but the size of your funeral is still going to depend on the weather.
Chuck Tanner, Pittsburgh Pirates manager, 1978

People have the most fun when they're busting their ass.
Ted Turner, Atlanta Braves owner, 1978

Either lead, follow or get out of the way.   **Ted Turner, 1980**

Progress always involves risks. You can't steal second base and keep your foot on first.
Frederick B. Wilcox, *Unicorns and Tadpoles*, 1980

You can't have dissension if you want to be in contention.
George Foster, Cincinnati Reds outfielder, 1981

Baseball is like driving. It's the one who gets home safely that counts.   **Tom Lasorda, Los Angeles Dodgers manager, 1981**

The worst curse in life is unlimited potential.
Ken Brett, Kansas City Royals pitcher, 1981

The body manifests what the mind harbors.
Jerry Augustine, Milwaukee Brewers pitcher, 1981

I've seen the future and it's much like the present, only longer.
Dan Quisenberry, Kansas City Royals pitcher, 1981

Ain't no sense in worrying about things you got control over, 'cause if you got control over them, ain't no sense worrying. And there ain't no sense worrying about things you got no control over, 'cause if you got no control over them, ain't no sense worrying.
Mickey Rivers, Texas Rangers outfielder, 1982

Chapter 28

Pitching

Let him hit it—you've got fielders behind you.
Alexander Cartwright, organized-baseball pioneer, 1846

What do you want me to do? Let them sons of bitches stand up there and think on my time?
Grover Cleveland Alexander,
when asked why he pitched so fast

How dumb can the hitters in this league get? I've been doing this for *fifteen* years. When they're batting with the count two balls and no strikes, or three and one, they're always looking for the fastball. And they *never* get it.
Eppa Rixey, Cincinnati Reds pitcher, 1927

My three pitches: my change, my change off my change, and my change off my change off my change.
Preacher Roe, Pittsburgh Pirates pitcher

Son, I think maybe we've had our workout for the day, don't you?

Bucky Harris, Washington Senators manager,
after his pitcher walked the first seven batters, 1942

That's the difference between a champ and a knife thrower. The champ may have lost his stuff temporarily or permanently, he can't be sure. When he can no longer throw his high hard one, he throws his heart instead. He throws something. He just doesn't walk off the mound and weep.

Raymond Chandler, novelist, letter to a friend, 1950

I throw the ball right down the middle. The high-ball hitters swing over it and the low-ball hitters swing under it.

Saul Rogovin, Chicago White Sox pitcher, 1952

The relief pitcher is the one man on a team that can make a manager look like a genuis.

Birdie Tebbets, Cincinnati Reds manager

Good pitching will always stop good hitting and vice-versa.

Casey Stengel, New York Yankees manager

I got good stamina, I got good wind, and the heat ain't got me, but I just don't have a good fastball.

Preacher Roe, Brooklyn Dodgers pitcher,
when his manager asked him how he felt, 1954

All pitchers are liars and crybabies.

Yogi Berra, New York Yankees catcher

How can a pitcher that wild stay in the league?

Yogi Berra, after fanning on three bad pitches

Sometimes the first sign a relief pitcher gets from the catcher is to wipe the mustard off his mouth.

Joe Garagiola, *Baseball Is a Funny Game*, 1960

That's all you pitchers talk about—runs, runs, runs!

Don Blasingame, Cincinnati Reds infielder, 1961

The pitcher is the happiest with his arm idle. He prefers to dawdle in the present, knowing that as soon as he gets on the mound and starts his windup he delivers himself to the uncertainty of the future.

George Plimpton, *Out of My League*, 1961

The best pitchers have the worst moves to first base, probably because they let so few runners get there.

Tommy Harper, California Angels outfielder

To a pitcher, a base hit is the perfect example of negative feedback. **Steve Hovley, Seattle Pilots pitcher, 1969**

I wish I were still active in baseball. The designated-hitter rule was made for me.

Dean Chance, former pitcher and lifetime .066 hitter, 1976

How can I intimidate batters, if I look like a goddamn *golf pro*.

Al Hrabosky, St. Louis Cardinals pitcher, on being ordered to shave his facial hair, 1977

This winter I'm working out every day, throwing at a wall. I'm eleven-and-oh against the wall.

Jim Bouton, former pitcher, planning a comeback, 1978

A lot of relief pitchers develop a crazy facade, and it's this facade that helps them deal with the pressure. Of course, maybe it's only the crazies that want to be relief pitchers.

Skip Lockwood, New York Mets relief pitcher, 1978

When you start thinkin' is when you get your ass beat.

Sparky Lyle, New York Yankees relief pitcher, 1978

Why pitch nine innings when you can get just as famous pitching two? **Sparky Lyle**

Most pitchers ought to have "For Display Purposes Only" on their bat. **Joe Garagiola, broadcaster, 1979**

I dunno. My eyes were closed.
Tommy Boggs, Atlanta Braves pitcher,
asked what he hit for a home run, 1981

I had Rick Burleson's bat. I had Buddy Bell's gloves. I had Tom Paciorek's helmet. All I needed was somebody's stroke.
Dave Stieb, Toronto Blue Jays pitcher,
forced to bat for himself in the All-Star Game, 1981

Once I tried to drown myself with a shower nozzle after I gave up a homer in the ninth. I found out you can't.
Dan Quisenberry, Kansas City Royals pitcher, 1981

If you think long, you think wrong.
Jim Kaat, Minnesota Twins pitcher, 1981

A lot of long relievers are ashamed to tell their parents what they do. The only nice thing about it is that you get to wear a uniform like everybody else.
Jim Bouton, former pitcher, 1981

I know you're throwing strikes, but why don't you mix in a ball once in a while?
Art Fowler, Oakland A's coach,
to his shell-shocked pitcher on the mound, 1981

The two most important things in life are good friends and a strong bull pen.
Bob Lemon, New York Yankees manager, 1981

Tom Griffin will be facing the heart of the order. Well, maybe not the heart, maybe the kidneys.
Hank Greenwald, San Francisco Giants announcer, 1981

Pitchers . . . always think that the ball has been secretly doctored to their disadvantage. This is nonsense. Everybody knows that pitchers are crazy.
Roger Angell, *Late Innings*, 1982

Len Barker (1976–)

When I see Barker watching a plane going overhead when he's on the mound, I know he's through.

Gabe Paul, Cleveland Indians president, 1980

Tell Len I'm very proud of him. I hope he does better next time.

**Mrs. Tokie Lockhart,
after her grandson pitched a perfect game, 1981**

Rex Barney (1943–50)

Rex Barney would be the league's best pitcher if the plate were high and outside. **Bob Cooke, sportswriter**

Bo Belinsky (1962–70)

When anything goes wrong around here, Belinsky, you're the first one I suspect.

Paul Richards, Los Angeles Angels coach, 1962

If I'd known I was gonna pitch a no-hitter today I would have gotten a haircut.

Bo Belinsky, Los Angeles Angels pitcher, 1962

I thought the only thing you ever did in the minors was chase broads. When did you have time to learn how to pitch?

**Steve Barber, Los Angeles Angels pitcher,
to Belinsky, 1962**

How can a guy win a game if you don't give him any runs?

**Bo Belinsky, as he was getting shelled,
15–0, in the seventh inning, 1963**

Christ, you want to talk about Bo Belinsky? I've been trying to forget the guy for six years.

Gene Mauch, Montreal Expos manager, 1972

Jim Brosnan (1954–63)

You got a sneaky fastball. . . . It doesn't look as fast as it actually is. Or maybe it looks faster than it actually is.
Gene Green, St. Louis Cardinals catcher, 1958

He hit a hanging slider. It was all I had. He missed the first two hanging sliders. **Jim Brosnan, on a home-run pitch, 1962**

Lew Burdette (1950–67)

Burdette would make coffee nervous.
Fred Haney, Milwaukee Braves manager, 1958

I make my living off the hungriness of the hitter.
Lew Burdette, 1961

William Burns (1908–12)

He followed two simple rules on the bench—on days he didn't pitch, he slept through the game; on days he did pitch, he slept only between innings. **Thomas P. Shea, sportswriter**

Clay Carroll (1964–78)

Clay Carroll buying a Lincoln Continental is like putting earrings on a hog.
Tommy Helms, Cincinnati Reds infielder, 1970

Steve Carlton (1965–)

Sometimes I hit him like I used to hit Koufax, and that's like drinking coffee with a fork! Did you ever try that?
Willie Stargell, Pittsburgh Pirates infielder, 1975

When Steve and I die, we are going to be buried in the same cemetery, sixty feet, six inches apart.
Tim McCarver, Philadelphia Phillies catcher, 1976

The two best pitchers in the National League don't speak English—Fernando Valenzuela and Steve Carlton.

> **Ernie Johnson, Atlanta Braves announcer,**
> **on Carlton's reluctance to speak to the press, 1981**

Jim Coates (1956–67)

Coates would knock you down whether you were black *or* white.

> **Whitey Ford, New York Yankees pticher,**
> **asked about racism on the team**

Jim Coates . . . could pose as the illustration for an undertaker's sign. He has a personality to match.

> **Jim Bouton, *Ball Four*, 1970**

Roger Craig (1955–66)

He pitched all that time with a team like that behind him? Well, he sure as hell deserves a lot more than a raise. He ought to bargain for a piece of the ball park.

> **Jimmy Hoffa, Teamsters president,**
> **upon hearing that Craig pitched 233 innings**
> **for the New York Mets, 1963**

You're standing on two tons of dirt. Why don't you rub some of it on the ball?

> **Casey Stengel, New York Mets manager,**
> **when Craig was having trouble holding onto the ball, 1962**

Mike Cuellar (1959–77)

Mike always thinks two pitches ahead. When they make an out on one of his "set-up" pitches, he looks like they've spoiled his fun. **Elrod Hendricks, Baltimore Orioles catcher**

I have given Mike Cuellar more chances than my first wife.

> **Earl Weaver, Baltimore Orioles manager, after**
> **Cuellar got knocked out in thirteen straight starts, 1976**

Dizzy Dean (1930–47)

If I'd have known his head was there, I would have thrown the ball harder.

**William Rogell, Detroit Tigers shortstop,
after he hit Dean on the forehead in the World Series, 1934**

The Good Lord was good to me. He gave me a strong body, a good right arm and a weak mind.

Dizzy Dean, at his Hall of Fame induction, 1953

If Diz ever gets smart, he's through.

**Paul Richards, Baltimore Orioles manager,
on Dean's country charm**

Luck? If the roof fell in and Diz was sitting in the middle of the room, everybody else would be buried and a gumdrop would drop in his mouth.

Leo Durocher, *Nice Guys Finish Last*, 1975

Al Downing (1961–77)

If Al were dining alone, he'd still use his butter knife.

Steve Garvey, Los Angeles Dodgers infielder

Moe Drabowsky (1956–72)

I didn't see it but it sounded low.

**Jim King, Chicago Cubs outfielder,
taking a Drabowsky fastball, 1956**

Moe, look around you. Where the fuck you gonna put him?

**Fred Hutchinson, Cincinnati Reds manager,
when Drabowsky had the bases loaded and
a three-ball count on the batter, 1962**

Don Drysdale (1956–69)

The trick against Drysdale is to hit him before he hits you.

Orlando Cepeda, San Francisco Giants infielder

I hated to bat against Drysdale. After he hit you, he'd come around, look at the bruise on your arm and say, "Do you want me to sign it?" **Mickey Mantle, former outfielder, 1981**

Ryne Duren (1954–69)

Whenever he came into a game people would stop eating their popcorn. **Casey Stengel, New York Yankees manager**

Ryne Duren was a one-pitch pitcher. His one pitch was a wild warm-up. **Jim Bouton, *Ball Four*, 1970**

Bob Feller (1936–56)

Go up and hit what you see. If you don't see anything, come on back.
**Bucky Harris, Washington Senators manager,
to hitters facing Feller**

Rollie Fingers (1968–   )

A fellow has to have faith in God above and Rollie Fingers in the bullpen. **Alvin Dark, Oakland A's manager, 1974**

Fingers has thirty-five saves. Rollie has a better record than John the Baptist.
Lon Simmons, San Francisco Giants announcer, 1978

Rollie will be the first relief pitcher inducted into the Hall of Fame—but not for his disposition.
Jerry Coleman, San Diego Padres manager, 1981

Bob Gibson (1959–75)

Gibson's the luckiest pitcher I've ever seen. Because he always picks the night to pitch when the other team doesn't score any runs. **Tim McCarver, Montreal Expos catcher, 1972**

When I got my glasses on, I can see a gnat pissin' in a piece of cotton.   **Bob Gibson, 1974**

Bob wasn't just unfriendly when he pitched. I'd say it was more like hateful.   **Joe Torre, New York Mets manager, 1981**

Lefty Gomez (1930–43)

Gomez, it took you ten years to get to third base and now you want to louse it up. Stay there.

> **Art Fletcher, New York Yankees coach,**
> **when Gomez wanted to steal home, 1935**

I know they're loaded. Did you think I thought they gave me another infield?   **Lefty Gomez, to his manager on the mound**

A lot of things run through your head when you're going in to relieve in a troubled spot. One of them was, "Should I spike myself?"   **Lefty Gomez**

Goose Gossage (1972–   )

There's smoke coming out of his nose and his cap is down over his eyes, and he's so big and hulking. You need a cape to face Gossage, not a baseball bat.

> **Tom Paciorek, Seattle Mariners infielder, 1981**

He can make the ball look so small that you're not even sure there's a practical purpose for being up there.

> **John Lowenstein, Baltimore Orioles outfielder, 1981**

Sometimes it sinks a little, sometimes it comes at you. At that speed, it does enough.

> **Carl Yastrzemski, Boston Red Sox outfielder, 1981**

The Goose should do more pitching and less quacking.

> **George Steinbrenner, New York Yankees owner, 1982**

Ross Grimsley (1971–   )

He is said to have enough greasy kid stuff in his ultra-long curly hair to give A. J. Foyt a lube job and an oil change.

Thomas Boswell, *Inside Sports*, 1981

Lefty Grove (1928–41)

He could throw a lamb chop past a wolf.

Arthur "Bugs" Baer, sportswriter

Ron Guidry (1975–   )

If there's anybody you can get out, tell me, and I'll let you pitch to him.

**Billy Martin, New York Yankees manager,
as Guidry was struggling, 1977**

My eyes tell me you can throw, the reports tell me you are a great prospect and the other clubs tell me they want you. How can so many people be wrong?

Gabe Paul, New York Yankees president, 1977

If you saw that pitching too often, there would be a lot of guys doing different jobs.

**Joe Rudi, California Angels outfielder,
after Guidry found his form, 1978**

What we need is Guidry and three days of rain.

Sparky Lyle, New York Yankees pitcher, 1978

Luke Hamlin (1933–44)

Hamlin is so wild, if he fell off the Brooklyn Bridge, he would not hit the water.   **Tom Meany, sportswriter**

He came into spring training as a hurricane and left as a gentle breeze.   **Jimmy Cannon, sportswriter**

Ed Hanyzewski (1942–46)

I liked to have broken my jaw tryin' to pronounce that one. But I said his name just by holdin' my nose and sneezing.

Dizzy Dean, broadcaster

Waite Hoyt (1918–38)

What's the matter with you? Other pitchers win their games 9–3, 10–2. You win yours 2–1, 1–0. Why don't you win your games like the others?

Jacob Ruppert, New York Yankees owner, 1927

The secret of success as a pitcher lies in getting a job with the Yankees.   **Waite Hoyt, 1927**

Carl Hubbell (1928–43)

Are you trying to insult Hubbell—coming up here with a bat?

**Gabby Hartnett, umpire,
as pitcher Lefty Gomez strode to the plate, 1934**

During the reign of Hubbell, first base itself was a marathon route.   **Heywood Broun, *New York World***

Tommy John (1963–   )

A lot of people say he may have a doctor's degree as far as baseballs are concerned.   **Don Drysdale, broadcaster, 1980**

Ask him the time and he'll tell you how to make a watch.

Bob Lemon, New York Yankees manager, 1980

Walter Johnson (1907–27)

There's only one way to time Johnson's fastball. When you see the arm start forward—swing.

Birdie McCree, New York Highlanders executive, 1908

Keep it. I don't want it.

> Ray Chapman, Cleveland Indians infielder, when told
> he had another strike coming against Johnson, 1915

He could throw the ball by you so fast you never knew whether you'd swung under it or over it.

> Smokey Joe Wood, former pitcher, 1979

Sandy Koufax (1955–66)

Either he throws the fastest ball I've ever seen, or I'm going blind.   Richie Ashburn, New York Mets outfielder, 1962

Show me a guy who can't pitch inside and I'll show you a loser.   Sandy Koufax

I can see how he won twenty-five games. What I don't understand is how he lost five.

> Yogi Berra, on Koufax' 1963 season of 25–5

We need just two players to be a contender. Just Babe Ruth and Sandy Koufax.

> Whitey Herzog, Texas Rangers manager, 1973

A foul ball was a moral victory.

> Don Sutton, Houston Astros pitcher, 1981

Don Larsen (1953–67)

The only thing he fears is sleep.

> Jimmy Dykes, Baltimore Orioles manager, 1954

He did it with a tremendous assortment of pitches that seemed to have five forward speeds, including a slow one that ought to have been equipped with backup lights.

> Shirley Povich, on Larsen's perfect World Series game,
> *Washington Post*, 1956

He was either out pretty late or up pretty early.
>   **Casey Stengel, New York Yankees manager, after Larsen clobbered a telephone pole with his car at 5:00 A.M., 1956**

Bill Lee (1969–)

It's a lot easier when you're starting because when you're starting you can pick your days to drink.   **Bill Lee, 1980**

He sounds a lot funnier when he's winning.
>   **Dick Williams, Montreal Expos manager, 1980**

I met him on the space shuttle.
>   **Lon Simmons, Oakland A's announcer, 1981**

Ed Lopat (1944–55)

Lopat looks like he is throwing wads of tissue paper. Every time he wins a game, fans come down out of the stands asking for contracts.   **Casey Stengel, New York Yankees manager**

Sal Maglie (1945–58)

He is the only man I've ever seen pitch a shutout on a day when he had absolutely nothing. Pitchers have those days . . . Maglie got by on meanness.
>   **Alvin Dark, *When in Doubt, Fire the Manager,* 1980**

Renie Martin (1979–)

Some people throw to spots, some people throw to zones. Renie throws to continents.
>   **Dan Quisenberry, Kansas City Royals pitcher, 1981**

Christy Mathewson (1900–16)

Mathewson pitched against Cincinnati yesterday. Another way of putting it is that Cincinnati lost a game of baseball. The first statement means the same as the second.

Damon Runyon, writer

Stu Miller (1952–68)

Boys, there's the first pitcher I ever saw that changed speeds on his change-up.

Dusty Rhodes, New York Giants outfielder

Van Lingle Mungo (1931–45)

Mungo and I get along fine. I just tell him I won't stand for no nonsense—and then I duck.

Casey Stengel, Brooklyn Dodgers manager

Sam McDowell (1961–75)

McDowell only throws a fastball. If that doesn't work he throws a faster one.   **Ron Smith, *True*, 1969**

Trying to think with me is a mismatch. Hell, most of the time I don't know where the pitch is going.

Sam McDowell, 1972

In his salad days, Sam McDowell drank more highballs than he pitched.   **Bucky Walter, *San Jose Mercury*, 1981**

Tug McGraw (1965–   )

Some persons go through life accident-prone; McGraw goes through life disaster-prone.   **Joseph Durso, sportswriter, 1974**

Some days you tame the tiger. And some days the tiger has you for lunch.   **Tug McGraw, on relief pitching, 1980**

Phil Niekro (1964–)

I just take my three swings and go sit on the bench. I don't even want to mess up my swing.

Dick Allen, Philadelphia Phillies infielder, on hitting Niekro's knuckleball

Trying to hit him is like trying to eat Jello with chopsticks.
Bobby Murcer, San Francisco Giants outfielder

It was great. I got to meet a lot of important people. They all sit behind home plate.

Bob Uecker, on catching Niekro's knuckleball, 1981

Satchel Paige (1948–63)

I've heard about Satchel throwing pitches that wasn't hit but that never showed up in the catcher's mitt, nevertheless.

Biz Mackey, Negro-leagues catcher

If Satch and I were pitching on the same team, we'd cinch the pennant by July 4th and go fishing until World Series time. **Dizzy Dean, St. Louis Cardinals pitcher, 1934**

His fastball sawed off bats at the *top*. **Dizzy Dean**

He threw the ball as far from the bat and as close to the plate as possible. **Casey Stengel, New York Yankees manager**

He threw me his arms, his elbows, his foot and his wrist, everything but the ball. The next thing I knew he threw the ball . . . to my surpise.

Eddie Yost, Washington Senators infielder

I could nip frosting off a cake with my fastball.
Satchel Paige, *Maybe I'll Pitch Forever*, 1962

Throw strikes. Home plate don't move. **Satchel Paige**

Jim Palmer (1965–   )

Cakes [Palmer] has won 240 games, but it took a picture of him standing in his underwear to get nationally known.

**Mike Flanagan, Baltimore Orioles pitcher,
on Palmer's Jockey commercials, 1981**

There's only one cure for what's wrong with all of us pitchers, and that's to take a year off. Then, after you've gone a year without throwing, quit altogether.

Jim Palmer, on sore arms, 1982

Gaylord Perry (1962–   )

Gaylord Perry has been approached by every investment firm in San Francisco. After all, he's the man who took a 39-cent jar of Vaseline and made himself a $100,000 pitcher.

Bob Bolin, Boston Red Sex pitcher, 1972

Everybody thinks that all the places he touches are decoys. I don't think any are decoys. I think he's got that stuff everywhere.

**George Bamberger, Milwaukee Brewers manager,
on Perry's greaseball, 1981**

Gaylord is a very honorable man. He only calls for the spitball when he needs it.

Gabe Paul, Cleveland Indians president, 1982

He should be in the Hall of Fame, with a tube of K-Y jelly attached to his plaque.

Gene Mauch, California Angels manager, 1982

These guys are so young they don't know I'm an ass.

Gaylord Perry, on his Seattle Mariners teammates, 1982

300 Wins is Nothing to Spit At.

**Gaylord Perry's T-shirt on
the day he won his 300th game, 1982**

Jack Quinn (1909–33)

He belonged to that venerable pitchers' union that called the dirt circling the mound the extent of their fielding range.

Fresco Thompson, *Every Diamond Doesn't Sparkle*, 1964

Bugs Raymond (1904–11)

What a terrific spitball pitcher he was. Bugs drank a lot. He didn't spit on the ball: He blew his breath on it, and the ball would come up drunk. **Rube Marquard, former pitcher, 1965**

Steve Rogers (1973–)

He's a sinkerball pitcher, and like all things that sink, they tend to get wet once in a while.

Ron Luciano, former umpire, 1981

Nolan Ryan (1966–)

He's baseball's exorcist—scares the devil out of you.

Dick Sharon, Detroit Tigers outfielder, 1974

Everybody's so sensitive, you'd think Nolan Ryan was pitching.

**Thurman Munson, New York Yankees catcher,
on his teammates during batting practice, 1979**

If you let him get a head of steam by the seventh inning, you can't hit him. You can't even *see* him.

Larry Sherry, California Angels pitching coach, 1979

Johnny Sain (1942–55)

Sain don't say much, but that don't matter much, because when you're out there on the mound, you got nobody to talk to.

Casey Stengel, New York Yankees manager, 1953

Tom Seaver (1967–   )

The owners think if I wasn't in baseball I'd be out digging ditches, or something. That really fries me. How can they be in baseball and not see what it's all about? Pitching is a beautiful thing. It's an art.

**Tom Seaver, on his contract problems
with M. Donald Grant of the New York Mets, 1977**

Blind people come to the park just to listen to him pitch.
Reggie Jackson, New York Yankees outfielder, 1977

When Seaver laughs, he makes dogs whine.
**Lindsey Nelson, San Francisco Giants announcer,
on Seaver's high-pitched laugh, 1981**

Bob Shaw (1957–67)

I've got to find out whether he is the lousiest lay in the world or the cheapest son of a bitch in baseball. Why else wouldn't a girl date him twice?

**Al Lopez, Chicago White Sox manager,
on Shaw's playboy reputation**

Warren Spahn (1942–65)

Hitting is timing. Pitching is upsetting timing.   **Warren Spahn**

A pitcher needs two pitches—one they're looking for and one to cross 'em up.   **Warren Spahn**

Spahn and Sain and two days of rain.
**Gerry Hearn, sportswriter, on Spahn and Johnny Sain,
linchpins of the Boston Braves' pitching staff, 1948**

I don't think Spahn will ever get into the Hall of Fame. He'll never stop pitching.

Stan Musial, St. Louis Cardinals outfielder, 1963

I don't know if we're the oldest battery, but we're certainly the ugliest. **Yogi Berra, New York Mets catcher, 1965**

Tracy Stallard (1960–66)

At the end of the season, they're gonna tear this joint down. The way you're pitchin', that right-field section will be gone already. **Casey Stengel, New York Mets manager, on the Polo Grounds, 1963**

Don Stanhouse (1972–)

Don Stanhouse . . . holds the ball so long he appears to be hoping the batter will fall victim to some crippling disease.
Art Hill, *I Don't Care if I Never Come Back*, 1980

Fred Talbot (1963–70)

I wouldn't want to fight him. As far as he's concerned the Marquis of Queensberry is some fag hairdresser.
Jim Bouton, *Ball Four*, 1970

Dizzy Trout (1939–57)

He came by his nickname quite naturally.
Irv Haag, sportswriter

Fernando Valenzuela (1980–)

When you're up there, it looks like you can hit him. Then it's like, "Here it is . . . no it ain't."
Bobby Bonds, Chicago Cubs outfielder, 1981

Watching Fernando Valenzuela force himself into a Los Angeles Dodgers uniform is something like seeing Kate Smith struggling to fit into a pair of Brooke Shields' designer jeans.
H. G. Reza, *San Francisco Chronicle*, 1981

He wants Texas back.

**Tom Lasorda, Los Angeles Dodgers manager,
on what Valenzuela wants for his contract, 1982**

Fernando Valenzuela apparently wants to be paid by the pound. **Furman Bisher, *The Sporting News*, 1982**

Rube Waddell (1897–1910)

Fact is, I've got so much speed today, I'll burn up the catcher's glove if I don't let up a bit.

**Rube Waddell, as he dipped his
arm in ice water to slow himself down**

When Waddell had control—and some sleep—he was un-beatable. **Branch Rickey, former St. Louis Browns manager**

Rube Waddell . . . loved pitching, fishing and drinking. When he died, they found him in a gin-filled bathtub with three drunken trout. **Mike Royko, *Chicago Sun-Times*, 1981**

Ed Walsh (1904–17)

I think that ball disintegrated on the way to the plate and the catcher put it back together again. I swear, when it went past the plate it was just the spit went by.

Sam Crawford, former outfielder, 1965

Early Wynn (1939–63)

That son of a bitch is so mean he'd fucking knock you down in the dugout. **Mickey Mantle, New York Yankees outfielder**

The pitcher's mound is my office—a place when I conduct my business. **Early Wynn, 1957**

Chapter 29

Politics and Baseball

Baseball is the game for young Americans. Gold is a better game for old Americans. **William H. Taft, advising Ty Cobb**

Hot as hell, ain't it, Prez?
**Babe Ruth, New York Yankees outfielder,
upon meeting Calvin C. Coolidge at Yankee Stadium**

They are having what is called a filibuster in the Senate. It means that a man can get up and talk hours at a time, just to keep some bill from coming to vote. Imagine a ballplayer standing at bat and not letting the other side play. Why, they would murder him. **Will Rogers, columnist**

Next to religion, baseball has furnished a greater impact on American life than any other institution. **Herbert C. Hoover**

Our people don't mind being rationed on sugar and shoes, but those men in Washington will have to leave our baseball alone!

**Fiorello H. LaGuardia, New York mayor,
asking for the continuance of baseball during the war, 1942**

I honestly feel that it would be best for the country to keep baseball going. These players are a definite recreational asset to at least twenty million of their fellow citizens—and that, in my judgment, is thoroughly worthwhile.

**Franklin D. Roosevelt, his "Green Light Letter"
to keep baseball going during the war, 1942**

Baseball is the moral equivalent of war.

Branch Rickey, Brooklyn Dodgers president

You don't have to weigh 250 pounds to make good in baseball. And you don't have to be 6-foot-7, either. I like that. I was a little fellow myself. **Harry S. Truman**

I'd get me a bunch of bats and balls and sneak me a couple of umpires and learn them kids behind the Iron Curtain how to tote a bat and play baseball.

Dizzy Dean, broadcaster, on how to solve the Cold War

I told him [my friend] that I wanted to be a real major-league baseball player, a genuine professional like Honus Wagner. My friend said he'd like to be president of the United States. Neither of us got our wish. **Dwight D. Eisenhower**

Get the hell out of my way, I'm coming through! Do you hear me? Get out of my way!

**Ty Cobb, former outfielder,
demanding to play through President Eisenhower
at Augusta National Country Club**

I'd rather be the Yankees catcher than the president, and that makes me pretty lucky, I guess, because I could never be the president. **Yogi Berra, New York Yankees catcher**

The man who bats most often has the most opportunity to hit the most foul balls—the President has a chance to bat every day.   **Lyndon B. Johnson, 1968**

What the hell are cops doing on the field? I've never seen cops on the field before. They ought to be at the university where they belong.

> **Ralph Houk, Yankees manager, at a
> time of student unrest, 1969**

The thought immediately occurs to you as you walk into the cloakroom that Congress is afternoon baseball.

> **Jimmy Breslin, *How the Good Guys Finally Won*, 1975**

I watch a lot of baseball on radio.

> **Gerald R. Ford, "Monday Night Baseball," ABC-TV, 1978**

The game has a cleanness. If you do a good job, the numbers say so. You don't have to ask anyone or play politics. You don't have to wait for the reviews.

> **Sandy Koufax, former pitcher, 1979**

The reason that Jimmy Carter was at the World Series—let's be honest—was to get votes. And I don't mind that, but when he decided to fill Andrew Young's post with Willie Stargell, that was a little obvious.

> **Johnny Carson, "The Tonight Show," NBC-TV, 1979**

The box score always adds up; politics never does.

> **James Reston, *The New York Times*, 1979**

More than anything, it's a game of innocence. Politicians come and go, but they always get booed at the ball park.

> **Pete Hamill, New York *Daily News*, 1981**

Even when they lose, they got heart. That's why the people of Brooklyn love 'em so much. Now if only those crooked politicians running this borough had half the brains of those baseball players, we'd be in a lot better shape.

David Ritz,
The Man Who Brought the Dodgers Back to Brooklyn, 1981

Chapter 30

Records, Awards, and Statistics

A baseball fan has the digestive apparatus of a billy goat. He can—and does—devour any set of diamond statistics with insatiable appetite and then nuzzle hungrily for more.

Arthur Daley, sportswriter

Any minute, any day, some players may break a long-standing record. That's one of the fascinations about the game—the unexpected surprises.

Connie Mack, *My 66 Years in the Big Leagues*, 1950

I never keep a scorecard or the batting averages. I hate statics. What I got to know I keep in my haid.

Dizzy Dean, broadcaster

Most Valuable Player on the worst team ever? Just how did they mean that?

Richie Ashburn, former New York Mets outfielder, on winning the award, 1962

There's one record I hold: Most World Series on the most different teams for a right-handed third baseman who didn't switch-hit and who never played for the Yankees.

Heinie Groh, former infielder, 1966

You couldn't play on my Amazin' Mets without having held some kind of record, like one fella held the world's international all-time record for a pitcher getting hit on the ankles.

Casey Stengel, former New York Mets manager, 1967

I began soaking up baseball records like a sea sponge before I even knew what they meant. I like the way you could read *around* baseball without ever getting to the game at all.

Wilfrid Sheed, "My Passport Was at Shortstop," 1968

Statistics are like the bathing suit, revealing everything except what is important. **John Mosedale, *The Greatest of All*, 1974**

Baseball fans love numbers. They like to swirl them around their mouths like Bordeaux wine. **Pat Conroy, *Sport*, 1974**

This is the biggest thing that ever happened to me. When I'm old and have grandchildren, I can say I was on the other end of the 715th home run.

**Tom House, Atlanta Brave pitcher,
on catching Hank Aaron's home run in the bull pen, 1974**

You don't think Hemingway or Michelangelo would have been delighted to see their achievements surpassed, do you?

**Maury Wills, former infielder, on Lou Brock
breaking his single-season base-stealing record, 1974**

Statistics are about as interesting as first-base coaches.

Jim Bouton, former pitcher, 1978

Any person claiming to be a baseball fan who does not also claim to have invented the quickest, simplest and most complete method of keeping score probably is a fraud.

Thomas Boswell, *Washington Post*, 1979

There is no column on the scorecard heading "remarks."
Sidney Lansburgh, Jr., *Baltimore Evening Sun,* **1979**

Congratulations on breaking my record last night. I always thought the record would stand until it was broken.
**Yogi Berra, New York Yankees coach,
wiring Johnny Bench after Bench broke his record
for career home runs by a catcher, 1980**

Right now there are two very nervous people in the park: the pitcher and the official scorer.
**Lindsey Nelson, San Francisco Giants announcer,
as Jerry Reuss was seven outs away from a no-hitter, 1980**

They should take that stat and shove it.
**Phil Rizzuto, New York Yankees announcer,
on the game-winning RBI, 1980**

I had a speech ready but somewhere along in twenty-eight years it got lost.
**Johnny Mize, former infielder, inducted
into the Hall of Fame twenty-eight years after retiring, 1981**

Baseball fans are junkies, and their heroin is the *statistic.*
Robert S. Wieder, "In Praise of the Second Season," 1981

They can make 250 bats out of one good tree. How's that for a statistic, baseball fans?
**Andy Rooney, visiting the Louisville Slugger Company,
"60 Minutes," CBS-TV, 1981**

I'll take any way to get into the Hall of Fame. If they want a batboy, I'll go in as a batboy.
Phil Rizzuto, former infielder, 1981

Chapter 31

Rookies and Veterans

A young ballplayer looks on his first spring-training trip as a stagestruck young woman regards the theater. She can think only of the lobster suppers and the applause and the colored lights.   **Christy Mathewson,** *Pitching in a Pinch,* **1914**

Be home real soon, Mom, they're beginning to throw the curve.   **Ring Lardner, "Alibi Ike," 1915**

My father looked at the money, then glanced at my seven brothers and sisters. He couldn't contain himself. He said, "For five hundred dollars you can take the whole family."
    Joe Dugan, as a Philadelphia Athletics bonus baby, 1917

My boy, one small breeze doesn't make a windstorm.
        John McGraw, New York Giants manager,
        to a hot rookie in spring training, 1925

If I had done everything I was supposed to, I'd be leading the league in homers, have the highest batting average, have given $100,000 to the Cancer Fund and be married to Marie Osmond.

Clint Hurdle, Kansas City Royals rookie outfielder, 1978

When a rookie does well, it fouls up the manager's plans. So he lets you pitch until you have a bad inning. Then he can ship you out as planned. **Jim Bouton, former pitcher, 1979**

A bonus guy is a prospect, and the trainers rub his arms with a secret salve from India. A suspect—a guy like me—got his arm rubbed with Three-in-One oil.

Bo Belinsky, former pitcher, 1980

All ballplayers should quit when it starts to feel as if all the baselines run uphill.

Babe Ruth, New York Yankees outfielder, 1934

He would throw one so lazy, so soft, so absolutely devoid of stuff, that a handwriting expert sitting in the stands could have read Ford Frick's character from his signature on the ball.

George Kirksey, sportswriter, on Dizzy Dean pitching in the World Series in the twilight of his career, 1938

I'm throwing twice as hard as I ever did. It's just not getting there as fast.

Lefty Gomez, New York Giants pitcher, near the end of his career, 1942

They have smelled the roses when they were in full bloom.

Warren Brown, sportswriter, on ballplayers

First you forget names, then you forget faces, then you forget to zip up your fly, and then you forget to unzip your fly.

Branch Rickey, Brooklyn Dodgers president, on the stages of senility

You start chasing a ball and your brain immediately commands your body to "Run forward! Bend! Scoop up the ball! Peg it to the infield!" Then your body says, "Who, me?"

Joe DiMaggio, former outfielder, on when to quit

I'll never make the mistake of being seventy again.

Casey Stengel, upon being fired as New York Yankees manager for being too old, 1960

No one else in here is gettin' younger, and I'm the only one gettin' older.

Casey Stengel, New York Mets manager, asked again if he might retire, 1965

Only in sports do we let our works of art and working artists fade out like light bulbs while the claque rushes off in hot pursuit of the incandescence of a new one.

Jim Murray, *The Best of Jim Murray*, 1965

You spend a good piece of your life gripping a baseball and in the end it turns out that it was the other way around all the time.   **Jim Bouton, *Ball Four*, 1970**

My manager spent ten years trying to teach me a change of pace. At the end of my career that's all I had.

Lefty Gomez, former pitcher

You dumb hitters. By the time you know what to do, you're too old to do it.   **Ted Williams, former outfielder, 1976**

The goat ate the Bible with my birth certificate. That goat lived to be twenty-seven.

Satchel Paige, former pitcher, asked his reply if he had to testify in court as to his age, 1976

How old would you be if you didn't know how old you was?

Satchel Paige

Beside the tombstone when I die, they can hang out the Dodgers' home schedule. Then when people are in the cemetery visiting loved ones, they can say, "Let's go to Lasorda's grave and see if the Dodgers are at home or away."

> **Tom Lasorda, Los Angeles Dodgers manager, 1976**

This game is youth, y'know. I mean, it *is*. That's one thing that's wrong with it.   **Mark Fidrych, *No Big Deal*, 1977**

A ballplayer's active life was as short as a dog's but you didn't really need to care, because he didn't die, only the fable you had made of him; a new pup was warming up.

> **Edward Hoagland, *Harper's*, 1977**

It's a mere moment in a man's life between an All-Star Game and an old-timers' game.

> **Vin Scully, Los Angeles Dodgers announcer, 1978**

This game is too much fun to ever get too old to play it.

> **Tug McGraw, Philadelphia Phillies pitcher, 1980**

A ballplayer has two lives—the first is a fantasy, the second a return to reality.   **Thomas Boswell, *Inside Sports*, 1980**

I know I find myself a helluva lot better ballplayer since I quit playing.   **Joe Garagiola, broadcaster, 1980**

I don't have to worry about the curve ball anymore.

> **Hank Aaron, former outfielder, on his retirement, 1981**

I guess this is one of the few times when you get to see your own last rites.

> **Steve Stone, Baltimore Orioles pitcher,**
> **announcing his retirement, 1982**

Chapter 32

Spitters and Beanballs

The tradition of professional baseball has been agreeably free of charity. The rule is, "Do anything you can get away with."

Heywood Broun, *New York World,* **1923**

You all done? You comfortable? Well, send for the grounds-keeper and get a shovel because that's where they're gonna bury you.

Dizzy Dean, St. Louis Cardinals pitcher,
to a batter who dug in at the plate

It's getting so you can't even get a hit off either of the Deans without getting beaned the next time out.

Jimmy Wilson, Philadelphia Phillies manager,
on Dizzy and Paul Dean, 1935

I don't name them—I just throw them.

Rip Sewell, Pittsburgh Pirates pitcher,
asked what he called his new blooper pitch, 1942

My best pitch is one I do not throw.

Lew Burdette, Milwaukee Braves pitcher, on his spitball

I don't want to get to know the other guys too well. I might like them, and then I might not want to throw at them.
Sal Maglie, New York Giants pitcher

I'll just hit the dry side of the ball.
**Stan Musial, St. Louis Cardinals outfielder,
on how he would handle Preacher Roe's spitball**

I've got a right to knock down anybody holding a bat.
**Early Wynn, Cleveland Indians pitcher,
after dusting his son**

I don't, but neither does the batter.
**Elroy Face, Pittsburgh Pirates pitcher, asked if
he knows which way his forkball will break, 1960**

You may not believe this, but I was trying to knock him down with the pitch. That shows you the kind of control I had that night.
**Paul Foytack, Los Angeles Angels pitcher,
on a pitch to Cleveland's Larry Brown, who hit
the fourth of four consecutive home runs off Foytack, 1963**

Reduce the load of juice, Gaylord, [umpire Ed] Sudol's getting suspicious of that splashing sound in my mitt.
**Tom Haller, San Francisco Giants catcher,
to Gaylord Perry, 1964**

Pitching is the art of instilling fear.
Sandy Koufax, Los Angeles Dodgers pitcher

I throw fewer spitters than anyone in the league.
Dean Chance, Los Angeles Angels pitcher, 1965

When I pitched for the San Francisco Seals in 1921, I hit nineteen men. *On purpose.* No way to say how many I missed.
Lefty O'Doul, former pitcher, 1966

Look for the seams and then hit in-between them.
**Harmon Killebrew, Minnesota Twins infielder,
on how to hit the knuckleball**

I'm tired of losing in old-timers' games.
**Whitey Ford, former pitcher,
on why he scuffed up the ball in an old-timers' game, 1970**

A spitball, down and in.
**Hank Aaron, Atlanta Braves infielder, on his
home run against Gaylord Perry in the All-Star Game, 1972**

I'd rather try hitting a hummingbird than a knuckleball.
Pete Rose, Cincinnati Reds outfielder, 1970

I'd always have it in at least two places, in case the umpires
would ask me to wipe off one. I never wanted to be caught
out there without anything. It wouldn't be professional.
**Gaylord Perry, on where he keeps his lubricant,
Me and the Spitter, 1974**

If you can cheat, I wouldn't wait one pitch longer.
**George Bamberger, Baltimore Orioles coach,
to Ross Grimsley on the mound, 1975**

There are two theories on hitting the knuckleball. Unfortunately, neither of them works.
Charlie Lau, Kansas City Royals coach, 1976

It's like a butterfly with hiccups. If you don't have a long fly
swatter, you're in trouble.
**Willie Stargell, Pittsburgh Pirates infielder,
on the knuckleball, 1978**

Never on Sunday.
**Don Sutton, Los Angeles Dodgers pitcher,
asked if he scuffs up the ball, 1978**

If they knocked one of our guys down, I'd knock down two of theirs. If they knocked two of our guys down, I'd get four. You have to protect your hitters.

Don Drysdale, former pitcher, 1980

My mother told me never to put my dirty fingers in my mouth.

Don Drysdale, denying he threw spitballs

Sidearm pitchers don't get many breaks from the umpires. They think we are freaks, that we belong on paddy wagons, with lace wrapped around our faces. They think we should be whipped.

Dan Quisenberry, Kansas City Royals pitcher, 1980

The worst animal in the world for a left-handed batter is a sidearm left-hander who wears glasses, and has to wipe them clean just before he throws.   **Joe Garagiola, broadcaster, 1980**

When you have a good screwball, hitters don't like it. As soon as you throw enough of them, hitters start looking at ads about broadcasting school.   **Joe Garagiola, 1981**

Watching the knuckleball at work has been variously described as similar to watching paint dry, grass grow, or A. J. Foyt park his car.

Lindsey Nelson, San Francisco Giants announcer, 1980

My teammates have nicknamed me "Retriever." All I ever seem to be doing is going back to the screen.

Bruce Benedict, Atlanta Braves catcher,
on handling the knuckleball, 1981

I don't cheat out there—at least I don't get caught.

Milt Wilcox, Detroit Tigers pitcher, 1981

Cheating is baseball's oldest profession. No other game is so rich in skulduggery, so suited to it or so proud of it.

Thomas Boswell, on doctored balls, *Inside Sports*, 1981

The best way to hide the spitter is to fake all the tricky stuff—
Vaseline behind the knee or under the bill of your cap—then
just spit on your hand when they're looking at you. I never
did it any other way.

George Bamberger, Milwaukee Brewers manager, 1981

Four basic ones—fastball, curve, slider and change-up—plus
eight illegal ones.

Tommy John, New York Yankees pitcher,
asked how many pitches he has, 1981

The screwball's an unnatural pitch. Nature never intended a
man to turn his hand like that throwing rocks at a bear.

Carl Hubbell, former pitcher, 1982

Chapter 33

Sportswriters

A ballplayer has two reputations, one with the other players and one with the fans. The first is based on ability. The second the newspapers give him.

Johnny Evers, former infielder, 1925

Nothing on earth is more depressing than an old baseball writer. **Ring Lardner, writer**

I know of no subject, save perhaps baseball, on which the average American newspaper discourses without unfailing sense and understanding. **H. L. Mencken, writer**

I give 'em each a scoop, so that their bosses can't bawl the three of 'em out for writing the same piece.

Dizzy Dean, St. Louis Cardinals pitcher, explaining why he gave three different birthplaces to reporters, 1934

Let me do the worrying.
Joe McCarthy, New York Yankees manager, to sportswriters

Hell, if the game was half as complicated as some of these writers make out it is, a lot of us boys from the farm would never have been able to make a living at it.

Bucky Walters, Cincinnati Reds pitcher

I don't want to sit around like a burglar all day, waiting for it to get dark so I can go to work.

**Edward T. Murphy, on why he gave up baseball writing
with the advent of night games**

Keep your mouth shut, your ears open, your pants buttoned, your feet on the ground, and keep one eye on the clock.

**Jimmy Murphy, *Brooklyn Eagle* editor,
to new baseball writers**

The only way you can get along with newspapermen is to be like Dizzy Dean. Say something one minute and something different the next. **Hank Greenberg, Detroit Tigers outfielder**

Watch out for the writers. Don't tell them sons-o-bitches nothing. **Jim Turner, New York Yankees coach, to players**

Anyone who thinks he can run baseball without a daily paper, can't run baseball.

Walter O'Malley, Brooklyn Dodgers owner

San Francisco writers describe the baseball scene with all the precision of three-year-old children fingerpainting on the playroom wall. **Jim Brosnan, *The Long Season*, 1960**

A baseball writer's relationship with a ballplayer is a cop-and-crook relationship. . . . Let's face it, the average ballplayer considers the writer a spy.

Jimmy Cannon, *No Cheering in the Press Box*, 1967

What the hell do they need quotes for? They all saw the play.

Tommy Harper, Seattle Pilots outfielder, 1969

The sportswriter doesn't watch many baseball games. In the press box he is usually occupied by trivia, girl watching or writing a piece for *The Sporting News*.

Leonard Shecter, *The Jocks*, 1970

Now what in hell kind of question is that? It's guys like you who can take a perfectly good press conference and fuck it up!

Charles O. Finley, Oakland A's owner, to reporters, 1975

The Lord taught me to love everybody, but the last ones I learned to love were the sportswriters.

Alvin Dark, Oakland A's manager, 1975

In general, the reporters ask idiotic questions. Did you feel the pressure? Were you happy to be pitching? Baseball is too mystical to be codified in words.

John Eskow, *New Times*, 1978

Baseball is the best sport for a writer to cover, because it's *daily*. It's ongoing. You have to fill the need, write the daily soap opera.   **Peter Gammons, *Boston Globe* sportswriter, 1978**

Reggie [Jackson] once said that the only people he can relate to are the writers. That's because they're the only ones who benefit from hearing his crap.

Sparky Lyle, *The Bronx Zoo*, 1979

What's the capital of Nebraska? What's the square root of 697? Does a bear shit in the woods? What's the meaning of death? Tell us, Gather. Tell us something. Tell us anything. But hurry up. We've got deadlines.

**Marty Bell, parodying
reporters' questions in his novel, *Breaking Balls*, 1979**

What will happen to the women reporters on the road? Most of the women writers I've seen are girls I wouldn't cross the street to ask for a date.

Maury Allen, New York sportswriter, 1979

If Jesus Christ were to show up with his old baseball glove, some guys wouldn't vote for him. He dropped the cross three times, didn't he?

**Dick Young, on Willie Mays not receiving
a unanimous Hall of Fame vote, New York *Daily News*, 1979**

I hope somebody hits .400 soon. Then people can start pestering *that* guy with questions about the last guy to hit .400.

Ted Williams, former outfielder, 1980

A ballplayer could go to college and be a sportswriter. But what writer could be a ballplayer? And tell me this: What college did the twelve apostles go to?

**Billy Martin, Oakland A's manager,
defending players against a charge that they are dumb, 1981**

Chapter 34

Spring Training

Is there anything that can evoke spring—the first, fine days of April—better than the sound of the ball smacking into the pocket of the big mitt, the sound of the bat as it hits the horse hide?

**Thomas Wolfe, novelist, dinner speech,
Baseball Writers of America, 1938**

Baseball teams go south every spring to cripple their players. In the old days they only stayed a couple of weeks, and they couldn't get many of them hurt in that time, but, nowadays, they stay till they get them all hurt.   **Will Rogers, columnist**

Take those fellows over to that other diamond. I want to see if they can play on the road.

**Casey Stengel, New York Mets manager,
at training camp, 1963**

Mamie Van Doren is here to serve as my physical fitness director.

> **Bo Belinsky, Philadelphia Phillies pitcher,**
> **bringing his girlfriends to training camp, 1965**

A word about Florida. It's as flat as a barber shop quartet after midnight. It's surrounded by salt water and covered by fresh air. It's a great place if you're a mosquito. An *old* mosquito.

> **Jim Murray, *The Best of Jim Murray*, 1965**

That's the true harbinger of spring, not crocuses or swallows returning to Capistrano, but the sound of a bat on the ball.

> **Bill Veeck, Chicago White Sox owner, 1976**

It's the fans that need spring training. You gotta get 'em interested. Wake 'em up. Let 'em know that their season is coming, the good times are gonna roll.

> **Harry Caray, Chicago White Sox announcer, 1976**

In winter, I get cabin fever bad. I wish I had a tape recording of the sounds of batting practice.

> **Ray Miller, Baltimore Orioles pitching coach, 1979**

To walk out and feel your spikes in the grass is a good feeling.

> **Reggie Jackson, New York Yankees outfielder, 1980**

Bobo Newsom always held out just for exercise. He hated spring training.

> **Furman Bisher, *Atlanta Journal* sportswriter, 1980**

Spring training is like a cat with nine lives. A baseball player has X number of lives and each spring is the birth of a new life.   **Steve Garvey, Los Angeles Dodgers infielder, 1981**

Watching a spring training game is as exciting as watching a tree form its annual ring.   **Jerry Izenberg, sportswriter, 1981**

Don't tell me about the world. Not today. It's springtime, and they're knocking baseballs around fields where the grass is damp and green in the morning and the kids are trying to hit the curve ball.

> Pete Hamill, New York *Daily News*, 1981

In the beginning, there was no baseball. But ever since, there have been few beginnings as good as the start of a new baseball season. It is the most splendid time in sport.

> B. J. Phillips, *Time*, 1981

The average age in Sun City, Arizona, is deceased.

> Bob Uecker, Milwaukee Brewers announcer, 1982

Anyone who comes to spring training in February is, of course, an honorary old man. No one who is unwilling to smell, taste, see, touch, and feel as though for the first time or last belongs there.

> Thomas Boswell,
> *How Life Imitates the World Series*, 1982

Chapter 35

Television and Radio

They played two World Series games at the Polo Grounds this afternoon—the one I watched and the one broadcast by Graham McNamee. **Ring Lardner, sportswriter, 1922**

You know, John, it's very impolite to belch, especially over the mike, unless you excuse yourself. I done belched and I done excused myself, so let's go. Everything is hunky-dory.
**Dizzy Dean, St. Louis Cardinals announcer,
to colleague Johnny O'Hara**

You learn 'em English and I'll learn 'em baseball.
Dizzy Dean, to a grammar teacher

I don't know how our folks come off callin' this the "Game of the Week." There's a much better game—Dodgers and Giants —*over on NBC*. **Dizzy Dean, broadcasting on CBS television**

Open the window, Aunt Minnie, here she comes!
**Rosey Rowswell, Pittsburgh Pirates announcer,
whenever he felt a Pirate home run neared**

It's a beautiful day for a night game.
>> **Frankie Frisch, St. Louis Cardinals announcer**

We don't care who wins—as long as it's the Cubs.
>> **Bert Wilson, Chicago Cubs announcer**

Here's the old redbird up in the catbird seat.
>> **Red Barber, Brooklyn Dodgers announcer**

He was as wild as a chicken hawk on a frosty morning.
>> **Red Barber, on a wild pitcher**

Ya see, I said "fuck" to ruin his audio. Then when I started scratching my ass I was ruining his video. He ain't gonna ask me a question like that again.
>> **Casey Stengel, New York Yankees manager**
>> **after a reporter asked if his team choked**
>> **in the World Series, 1957**

How 'bout that.   **Mel Allen, New York Yankees announcer**

Give me the Hoover! Give me the Hoover!
>> **Bob Prince, Pittsburgh Pirates announcer,**
>> **asking for a double play**

What'll it be tonight, Howard? Do you bullshit me or do I bullshit you?
>> **Tracy Stallard, Boston Red Sox pitcher,**
>> **to Howard Cosell, thinking the microphone was off, 1961**

I've got mike fright. I'm like Joe Garagiola. *I'm* afraid of the mike. *He's* afraid he won't get it.
>> **Stan Musial, former outfielder, 1964**

Fastball, about cock-high.
>> **Steve Carlton, St. Louis Cardinals pitcher,**
>> **when asked on the air what the home-run pitch was, 1968**

It's a weird scene. You win a few baseball games and all of a sudden you're surrounded by reporters and TV men with cameras asking you about Viet Nam and race relations.

Vida Blue, Oakland A's pitcher, 1971

He talks very well for a guy who's had two fingers in his mouth all his life.

**Gene Mauch, Montreal Expos managers,
on suspected spitballer Don Drysdale,
new California Angels announcer, 1972**

Interviews were the hardest thing for me at first. I felt so damn funny asking players questions when I already knew the answers. **Don Drysdale, California Angels announcer, 1972**

You are the only announcer in the big leagues who keeps his job because of his arm instead of his voice.

**Al Michaels, Cincinnati Reds announcer,
to his color man, Joe Nuxhall, 1974**

He slides into second with a standup double.

Jerry Coleman, San Diego Padres announcer, 1978

I don't mind hate mail, but when a letter comes to the station addressed "Jerk, KSFO, San Francisco," and I get it, then I start to worry.

Lon Simmons, San Francisco Giants announcer, 1978

It was raining so hard three people were injured by buckets.

Lon Simmons, 1978

If the World Series goes seven games, it will be NBC's longest-running show this fall.

Johnny Carson, "The Tonight Show," NBC-TV, 1978

Holy cow!   **Phil Rizzuto, New York Yankees announcer**

Well, that kind of puts a damper on even a Yankees win.

Phil Rizzuto, on a bulletin
announcing that Pope Paul VI had died, 1978

All the writers, then all those guys who stick microphones in your face and then don't say anything. Maybe in some other town, I wouldn't feel that way. But I feel I'm overmatched in this neighborhood. It's after the games that bends my butt out of shape.

Bob Lemon, New York Yankees manager,
on New York media, 1979

If the World Series runs until election day, the networks will run the first one-half inning and project the winner.

Lindsey Nelson, San Francisco Giants announcer, 1980

I swear I haven't had this much attention since I was a baby.

Broderick Perkins, San Diego Padres outfielder,
leading the league in hitting, 1981

Kansas City and Cleveland, a doubleheader, was postponed because of rain. They'll play four tomorrow.

Hank Greenwald, San Francisco Giants announcer, 1981

Herndon seems to be bothered by insects at the plate. I don't know what species it is. Maybe it's an infield fly.

Hank Greenwald, 1981

If Cey had been wearing Howard Cosell's toupee, he never would have felt the pitch that hit him.

Johnny Carson, on the Goose Gossage beaning
of Ron Cey in the World Series, 1981

I heard that doctors revived a man after being dead for four-and-a-half minutes. When they asked what it was like being dead, he said it was like listening to New York Yankees announcer Phil Rizzuto during a rain delay.

David Letterman,
"Late Night with David Letterman," NBC-TV, 1982

We don't have the record on that. The only thing our producer has in the truck is a TV schedule, the A's press guide, and a Whiz Bang comic book.

Lon Simmons, Oakland A's announcer, 1982

The best show on television is Red Sox baseball. Everything else sucks.   **Stephen King, novelist, 1982**

Chapter 36

Umpires

The average umpire is a worthless loafer.
Chicago Tribune, editorial, 1880

The best recommendation for an umpire in the old days was:
"He licked somebody in the Three-I League. He ought to do."
Ty Cobb, *Bustin' Em and Other Big League Stories*, 1914

Many fans look upon an umpire as a sort of necessary evil to
the luxury of baseball, like the odor that follows an automobile.
Christy Mathewson, *Pitching in a Pinch*, 1914

Why do I like baseball? The pay is good, it keeps you out in
the fresh air and sunshine, and you can't beat them hours.
Tim Hurst, umpire

Call 'em fast and walk away tough.   **Tim Hurst**

Der ain't no close plays, me lad; dey is either dis or dat.
Bill Guthrie, umpire

Some of ours is so crooked that they can lay in a berth only when the train's making a curve.

Ring Lardner, on umpires, *Saturday Evening Post*, 1918

It ain't nothin' till I call it. **Bill Klem, umpire**

Maybe, but I wouldn't have if I had a bat.

Bill Klem, after Hack Wilson claimed that Klem missed a pitch

If the Pope was an umpire, he'd still have trouble with the Catholics. **Beans Reardon, umpire**

Oh, Hack, if the bat hits the ground, you're out of the game.

Beans Reardon, when Hack Wilson threw his bat in the air protesting a call

Somethin' like four thousand bottles have been thrown at me in my day but only about twenty ever hit me. That does not speak very well for the accuracy of the fans' throwing.

Harry "Steamboat" Johnson, *Standing the Gaff*, 1935

Don't fight with the umpires. You can't expect them to be as perfect as you are.

Joe McCarthy, New York Yankees manager

Boys, I'm one of those umpires that can make a mistake on the close ones. So if it's close, you'd better hit it.

Cal Hubbard, umpire

That's just your trouble. You've got 1-A ears and 4-F eyes. You hear everything everybody has to say but you don't see half the things you're supposed to see.

Fresco Thompson, Brooklyn Dodgers executive, to Chuck Solodare

You argue with the umpire because there's nothing else you *can* do about it. **Leo Durocher, Brooklyn Dodgers manager**

It is wonderful to be here, to be able to hear the baseball against the bat, ball against glove, the call of the vendor, and be able to boo the umpire.

General Douglas MacArthur, returning from Europe, 1946

Why, they shot the wrong McKinley.

Dizzy Dean, St. Louis Cardinals announcer, on umpire William McKinley, 1950

Quick to think. Slow to anger.

Warren Giles, National League president; his two fundamental instructions to umpires

Despite all the nasty things I have said about umpires, I think they're one hundred percent honest. But I can't for the life of me figure out how they arrive at some of their decisions.

Jimmy Dykes, Baltimore Orioles manager, 1954

In a way an umpire is like a woman. He makes quick decisions, never reverses them, and doesn't think you're safe when you're out.   **Larry Goetz, umpire, 1955**

The toughest call an umpire has to make is not the half-swing; the toughest call is throwing a guy out of the game after you blew the hell out of the play.   **Johnny Rice, umpire**

Yogi is the last of the playing umpires.

Joe Garagiola, on Yogi Berra, 1960

I occasionally get birthday cards from fans. But it's often the same message: they hope it's my last.

Al Forman, umpire, 1962

Anytime I got those "bang-bang" plays at first base, I called 'em out. It made the game shorter.   **Tom Gorman, umpire**

Now, what the hell. Do you think I'd admit that?

Augie Donatelli, umpire, asked if he had ever blown a call

How could he be doing his job when he didn't throw me out of the game after the things I called him?

**Mark Belanger, Baltimore Orioles infielder,
on umpire Russ Goetz**

The first guy who lays a finger on this blind old man is fined fifty bucks!

**Gene Mauch, Montreal Expos manager, when his
players rushed out to dispute a call**

Why is it that they boo me when I call a foul ball correctly and they applaud the starting pitcher when he gets taken out of the ballgame?   **Jerry Neudecker, umpire, 1969**

If they did get a machine to replace us, you know what would happen to it? Why, the players would bust it to pieces every time it ruled against them. They'd clobber it with a bat.

Harry Wendelstedt, umpire, 1974

What fuckin' umpire wants to be known as a nice guy? God-damn players, they think you're a nice guy, they'll shit all over you, that's why.   **Harry Wendelstedt, 1974**

They're all a bunch of crybabies, especially the small-change hitters.   **Doug Harvey, umpire, on players, 1974**

Listen, ump. How can you sleep with the lights on?

**Amos Otis, Kansas City Royals outfielder,
to an umpire at a night game**

I made a game effort to argue. . . . Two things were against me: the umpires and the rules.

Leo Durocher, *Nice Guys Finish Last*, 1975

The players are all creeps. Who the hell wants to spend any time with them anyway?

**Dick Stello, umpire,
on not being able to fraternize with players, 1975**

They expect an umpire to be perfect on opening day and to improve as the season goes on.   **Nestor Chylak, umpire, 1979**

I was down at third base checking out all the girls in the stands and I called a homer that was forty feet foul.
Ron Luciano, umpire, changing a call in Baltimore, 1980

The president of the league is the only guy who comes to the ballgame and roots for the umpires.
Hank Greenwald, San Francisco Giants announcer, 1981

Next to hangman, umpire is the most paranoid profession.
Lowell Cohn, *San Francisco Chronicle*, 1981

We went the whole game without going to the bathroom.
Jack Lietz, on his crew,
who umpired the longest game ever played, over eight hours,
between Rochester and Pawtucket, 1981

I was just telling the umpire that with the garbage I threw, I couldn't afford to have him make too many bad calls.
Jim Bouton, *Ball Four Plus Ball Five*, 1981

Umpires sleep with their eyes open.
Lon Simmons, Oakland A's announcer, 1982

Umpiring is best described as the profession of standing between two seven-year-olds with one ice cream cone.
Ron Luciano, *The Umpire Strikes Back*, 1982

Chapter 37

Utility Players and Trades

You have to improve your club if it means letting your own brother go.   **Joe McCarthy, New York Yankees manager**

He played first base and the outfield, pinch-hit, and did everything but collect tickets.

> **Casey Stengel, Boston Braves manager,**
> **on Tommy Byrne as a minor leaguer, 1942**

I broke in with four hits and the writers promptly decided they had seen the new Ty Cobb. It took me only a few days to correct that impression.   **Casey Stengel**

Trade a player a year too early rather than a year too late.

> **Branch Rickey, Brooklyn Dodgers president**

We played him and now we can't trade him.

> **Buzzie Bavasi, Brooklyn Dodgers general manager,**
> **on Don Zimmer, a play-me-or-trade-me- player, 1957**

Hells bells! I traded Schoendienst, I didn't kill him.

> Frank Lane, former general manager,
> on adverse fan reaction, 1961

If they moved that foul line thirty feet to the left I'd make 'em forget Babe Ruth.

> Gene Freese, Cincinnati Reds infielder, 1961

I'm in the twilight of a mediocre career.

> Frank Sullivan, Minnesota Twins pitcher, 1962

Managers and general managers are trying to trade a load of ashes for a load of coal.

> Fresco Thompson, on winter meetings,
> *Every Diamond Doesn't Sparkle*, 1964

You can't get rich sitting on the bench—but I'm giving it a try. Phil Linz, Philadelphia Phillies infielder, 1965

You mean I got traded for Dooley Womack? *The* Dooley Womack?

> Jim Bouton, pitcher,
> traded to the Houston Astros, 1969

They're going to retire my uniform—with me still in it.

> Steve Hovley, Oakland A's outfielder, 1971

I might have gone beyond it.

> Rocky Bridges, former infielder,
> asked if he felt he reached his potential, 1972

I'm not sure which is more insulting, being offered in a trade or having it turned down.

> Claude Osteen, Los Angeles Dodgers pitcher, 1973

Bench me or trade me.

> Chico Ruiz, Cincinnati Reds infielder,
> after his manager played him for two weeks, 1974

Sometimes the best deals are the ones you don't make.
> Bill Veeck, Chicago White Sox owner, 1976

Among all the men who play baseball there is, very occasionally, a man of such qualities of heart and mind and body that he transcends even the great and glorious game, and that such a man is to be cherished, not sold.
> A. Bartlett Giamatti,
> on Tom Seaver's sale by the New York Mets, *Harper's*, 1977

If I knew then what I know now, I wouldn't have made the trade. But if I knew what I know now, I wouldn't have voted for Richard Nixon.
> Hank Peters, Baltimore Orioles general manager,
> on trading for Reggie Jackson
> and losing him to free agency, 1978

I don't want to be a star. Stars get blamed for too much.
> Enos Cabell, Houston Astros infielder, 1978

The day I got a hit off Koufax was when he knew it was all over.
> Sparky Anderson, former infielder
> and lifetime .247 hitter, 1979

It's a lot more fun trading a player than signing him.
> Roland Hemond, Chicago White Sox general manager, 1980

Crumbs on another man's table may be a main course on mine.
> Charles O. Finley, Oakland A's owner, 1980

I was very calm. What are they going to do if I *don't* get a hit? Bench me?
> Bill Nahorodny, Atlanta Braves catcher,
> getting a key pinch hit after riding the bench
> the whole season, 1981

I went through life as the "player to be named later."
> Joe Garagiola, former catcher, 1981

He's seen a lot of action, all right, but he's seen it from the seat of his pants in the dugout.

**Hank Greenwald, San Francisco Giants announcer,
on Steve Swisher, 1981**

If they ever start an Instructional League Hall of Fame, I'll be a charter member.

David Clyde, former pitcher, 1982

You think Ron Davis isn't trying to get traded? He's done everything but light himself on fire at Minnesota.

Al Michaels, broadcaster, 1982

Chapter 38

Winning and Losing

In playing or managing, the game of ball is only fun for me when I'm out in front and winning. I don't care a bag of peanuts for the rest of the game.

John McGraw, New York Giants manager, 1903

It's tomorrow that counts. So you worry all the time. It never ends. Lord, baseball is a worrying thing.

Stanley Coveleski, Cleveland Indians pitcher

You got to get twenty-seven outs to win.

Casey Stengel, New York Yankees manager

There are 154 games in a season and you can find 154 reasons why your team should have won every one of them.

Bill Klem, umpire

We whipped Chicago twice. Nothing in the world could stop us now. Winning makes winning like money makes money.

Mark Harris, *Bang the Drum Slowly*, 1956

It's natural to feel it. But you hide it. Show it, and you are through.

    Joe Garagiola, on pressure, *Baseball Is a Funny Game,* **1960**

The Great American Game should be an unrelenting war of nerves.   **Ty Cobb,** *My Life in Baseball,* **1961**

A man who wakes up and finds himself a success has not been sleeping.

    Frank Lane, Kansas City Athletics general manager, 1961

Oh, hell, if you win twenty games they want you to do it every year.

    Billy Loes, San Francisco Giants pitcher, when asked why he'd never won twenty games in a season, 1961

Losing after great striving is the story of man, who was born to sorrow, whose sweetest songs tell of saddest thought.

    Roger Kahn, *The Boys of Summer,* **1971**

Win any way you can as long as you can get away with it.

    Leo Durocher, *Nice Guys Finish Last,* **1975**

Show me a good loser, and I'll show you an idiot.

    Leo Durocher

Baseball, so simple, so out-in-the-open, is only brought to its finest stage of appreciation when every detail, every slider low-and-away is studied in the midst of a crackling tension.

    Thomas Boswell, *Washington Post,* **1978**

Root only for the winner. That way you won't be disappointed.

    Tug McGraw, Philadelphia Phillies pitcher, 1978

I think the National League has better biorhythms in July.

    Earl Weaver, Baltimore Orioles manager, on why the National League always wins the All-Star Game, 1979

The sooner you fall behind, the more time you have to catch up. **Sam Ogden,** *Time,* **1979**

What do you mean, pressure? In New York, I pitched once when we were trying to keep from losing 100 games. That's pressure. **Nino Espinosa, former New York Mets pitcher, 1979**

There's a certain scent when you get close to winning. You may go a long time without winning, but you never forget that scent. **Steve Busby, Kansas City Royals pitcher, 1979**

Winning isn't everything. Wanting to win is.
                    Catfish Hunter, New York Yankees pitcher, 1979

When the pressure builds up, it's like being on a bus in a mudhole. The harder you press on the pedal, the further you sink in the mud.
                    Bob Watson, New York Yankees infielder, 1980

Creating success is tough. But keeping it is tougher. You have to keep producing, you can't ever stop. Not even to take a crap.
                    Pete Rose, Philadelphia Phillies infielder, 1980

In baseball, there's no such thing as a small enemy.
                    **Fernando Valenzuela, Los Angeles Dodgers pitcher,
                    on facing the Chicago Cubs, 1981**

The secret to keeping winning streaks going is to maximize the victories while at the same time minimizing the defeats.
                    John Lowenstein, Baltimore Orioles outfielder, 1982

Chapter 39

Wives and Family

Alimony is like buying oats for a dead horse.
                    Arthur "Bugs" Baer, baseball writer

No one is a pull hitter in the first year of marriage.
          Walker Cooper, St. Louis Cardinals catcher, 1945

It's got to be better than rooming with Joe Page.
          **Joe DiMaggio, New York Yankees outfielder,
          on his marriage to Marilyn Monroe, 1954**

Keep them apart and keep the club.
          **Casey Stengel, New York Yankees manager,
          on players' wives**

A man bites off more trouble than he can chew when he doesn't do what his wife wants. You better believe it.
          Satchel Paige, *Maybe I'll Pitch Forever*, 1962

There are only two groups of people in the world who have the last word: umpires and wives, and if you dispute either you can get thrown out of the game or your comfortable house with equal speed.

Fresco Thompson, *Every Diamond Doesn't Sparkle,* **1964**

They shouldn't throw at me. I'm the father of five or six kids.

Tito Fuentes, San Francisco Giants infielder

Okay, all you guys, act horny.

Jim Pagliaroni, Seattle Pilots catcher,
about to greet their wives after a road trip, 1969

Explaining to your wife why *she* needs a penicillin shot for *your* kidney infection.

Mike Hegan, Seattle Pilots catcher,
on the toughest thing in baseball, 1969

For most ballplayers, all getting married means is that now they have to *hide* their datebooks. **Don Kowet,** *Sport,* **1974**

My Turn at Bat Was No Ball.

Delores Williams, wife of Ted Williams;
her proposed book title

A wife is an economist in the kitchen, a lady in the parlor and a whore in the bedroom.

Johnny Bench, Cincinnati Reds catcher, 1980

The players are at home, hanging around with their wives. The big thing about that, it's going to produce a bigger father/son/daughter game next year.

Bob Uecker, broadcaster, on the players' strike, 1981

Marriage is a great institution—to a lot of women.

Ron Luciano, former umpire, 1980

Two years ago, I retired from baseball to be closer to my family. Last October my wife left me.

Jerry Grote, New York Mets catcher, 1981

It is hard to raise a family over the telephone.
>
> **Don Sutton, Houston Astros pitcher, 1981**

It was too bad I wasn't a second baseman; then I'd probably have seen a lot more of my husband.
>
> **Karolyn Rose, ex-wife of Pete Rose, 1981**

Dad, they're playing the baseball song again.
>
> **Mike Bouton, age seven, to his father Jim Bouton upon hearing "The Star-Spangled Banner," 1969**

It's a hard slider.
>
> **Allison Perry, age five, asked if her father Gaylord Perry throws a greaseball, 1971**

Get your shit over the plate. Get that damned shit over.
>
> **Petie Rose, age three, son of Pete Rose, when Dock Ellis asked where he wanted a pitch**

So all those people booing wouldn't know you were my father.
>
> **Shirlee Anderson, on why she booed her father Sparky Anderson during his playing career**

Chapter 40

World Series

My idea of the height of conceit would be a political speaker that would go on the air when the World Series is on.
Will Rogers, columnist

The gods decree a heavyweight match only once in a while and a national election only every four years, but there is a World Series with every revolution of the earth around the sun. And in between, what varied pleasure long drawn out!
Jacques Barzun, *God's Country and Mine*, 1954

If this damned thing doesn't start soon, I'm going to fly straight up into the air!
Curt Blefary, Baltimore Orioles outfielder, before the start of the World Series, 1966

The romance of baseball . . . is in its capacity for stirring fantasy. We are never too old or too bothered to see ourselves wrapping up a World Series victory with a homer in the final inning of the seventh game. **Ron Fimrite, *Way to Go*, 1979**

Not playing in a World Series for a great hitter is like not making the Met for a great singer, not playing the Old Vic for a great actor.   Jim Murray, *Los Angeles Times,* 1979

October. That's when they pay off for playing ball.
                    Reggie Jackson, New York Yankees outfielder, 1980

The World Series is American sport's annual ticket to a romantic yesterday, when we all were young and surely going to be in the big leagues some day.
                    Ray Fitzgerald, *The Sporting News,* 1981

Baseball is really two sports—the Summer Game and the Autumn Game. One is the leisurely pasttime of our national mythology. The other is not so gentle.
                    Thomas Boswell,
                    How Life Imitates the World Series, 1982

1919: Chicago White Sox vs. Cincinnati Reds

Advise all not to bet on this Series. Ugly rumors afloat.
                    Hugh Fullerton,
                    Chicago Herald and Examiner sportswriter,
         prior to the Series, wiring papers carrying his column, 1919

The eight of us did our best to kick it, and little Richie Kerr won the game by his pitching.
                    Shoeless Joe Jackson, Chicago White Sox outfielder,
                    on game three, which many felt was on the level, 1920

I done it for the wife and kiddies.
                    Eddie Cicotte, Chicago White Sox pitcher,
                    on why he took the money, 1920

As Jackson departed the Grand Jury room, a small boy clutched at his sleeve and tagged along after him. "Say it ain't so, Joe," he pleaded. "Say it ain't so." "Yes, kid, I'm afraid it is," Jackson replied.
                    Chicago Herald and Examiner, 1920

Benedict Arnolds! Betrayers of American boyhood. Not to mention American Girlhood and American Womanhood and American Hoodhood. **Nelson Algren, writer**

Arnold Rothstein is a man who waits in doorways . . . a mouse, waiting in the doorway for his cheese.
William J. Fallon, lawyer, on the World Series fixer, 1921

The Lord must have known when he made the world round that nothing in it would ever be on the square.
Eddie Cicotte, at age eighty-three, 1967

I enjoy watching football in the afternoon, one of the things I love about this country. Baseball, too. I've loved baseball ever since Arnold Rothstein fixed the World Series in 1919.
Hyman Roth, to Michael Corleone,
in *The Godfather, Part II*,
screenplay by Francis Ford Coppola and Mario Puzo, 1976

1945: Detroit Tigers vs. Chicago Cubs

I don't think either team is capable of winning.
Warren Brown, sports editor,
on the war-decimated lineups of both clubs, 1945

It is the fat men against the tall men at the annual office picnic.
Frank Graham, sportswriter,
on the many miscues during the Series, 1945

1952: New York Yankees vs. Brooklyn Dodgers

Too much spit on it.
Billy Loes, Brooklyn Dodgers pitcher,
on why he committed a crucial balk, 1952

There were fifty-five reasons why I shouldn't have pitched him, but fifty-six why I should.
Casey Stengel, New York Yankees manager,
on why he started Ed Lopat in game seven, 1952

You made an easy play look hard.
>**George Weiss, New York Yankees owner,**
>**on Billy Martin's dramatic catch in game seven**

1953: *New York Yankees vs. Brooklyn Dodgers*

I lost it in the sun.
>**Billy Loes, Brooklyn Dodgers pitcher,**
>**on why he misplayed a ground ball, 1953**

1954: *New York Giants vs. Cleveland Indians*

They shoulda thrown me changeups. I couldn't hit a changeup good, even if some Eskimo was pitching.
>**Dusty Rhodes, New York Giants outfielder,**
>**after he destroyed the Indians with key hits**

I don't compare them. I catch 'em.
>**Willie Mays, New York Giants outfielder, asked to**
>**compare his over-the-shoulder catch on Vic Wertz, 1954**

I want a new catcher. If somebody's going to set a record for passed balls in the World Series, I don't want it to be me.
>**Wes Westrum, New York Giants catcher,**
>**signaling in his manager after boxing around**
>**Hoyt Wilhelm's knuckleballs, 1954**

1956: *New York Yankees vs. Brooklyn Dodgers*

The million-to-one shot came in. Hell froze over. A month of Sundays hit the calendar. Don Larsen today pitched a no-hit, no-run, no-man-reach-first game in a World Series.
>**Shirley Povich, *Washington Post*, 1956**

Cripes, I've never seen so many managers.
>**Casey Stengel, New York Yankees manager,**
>**on his players during the ninth inning**
>**of Larsen's perfect game, 1956**

No, why should I?

> Don Larsen, asked if he ever gets tired
> talking about his perfect game

1960: Pittsburgh Pirates vs. New York Yankees

As Dr. Dafoe said when he handed the fourth Dionne baby to the nurse, "This thing ain't over yet." The 1960 World Series is going into the seventh game.

> Dick Young, *New York Daily News*, 1960

Forbes Field at this moment is an outdoor insane asylum!

> Jack Brickhouse, network announcer, as Hal Smith
> hit a three-run home run to give Pittsburgh
> a 9–7 lead in the eight inning of game seven, 1960

I sure hate to see it happen to you, but you sure took me off the hook.

> Jim Coates, New York Yankees pitcher,
> who was yanked for Ralph Terry,
> the man who gave up Bill Mazeroski's
> "shot heard 'round the world" in game seven, 1960

We made too many wrong mistakes.

> Yogi Berra, New York Yankees catcher,
> on why they lost, 1960

1963: Los Angeles Dodgers vs. New York Yankees

I had two great thrills in the World Series; when I thought it was over, and then when it actually was over.

> Sandy Koufax, Los Angeles Dodgers pitcher,
> after Dick Tracewski dropped what would have been
> the final out of the Series, 1963

1969: New York Mets vs. Baltimore Orioles

God is living in New York City, and he's a Mets fan.

> **Tom Seaver, New York Mets pitcher, 1969**

1975: Cincinnati Reds vs. Boston Red Sox

It's not often a mediocre pitcher gets to start in the sixth game of a World Series.

> **Bill Lee, Boston Red Sox pitcher,**
> **scheduled to start that day (he didn't)**

Can you believe this ballgame?

> **Pete Rose, Cincinnati Reds infielder, to Carlton Fisk**
> **during the eleventh inning of game six, 1975**

We're the best team in baseball. But not by much.

> **Sparky Anderson, Cincinnati Reds manager,**
> **at the conclusion of the Series, 1975**

It is 8–7, one out, and school will never start, rain will never come, sun will warm the back of your neck forever.

> **A. Bartlett Giamatti, educator and writer,**
> **on game six, 1980**

1977: New York Yankees vs. Los Angeles Dodgers

I must admit, when Reggie hit his third home run and I was sure nobody was looking, I applauded in my glove.

> **Steve Garvey, Los Angeles Dodgers infielder,**
> **after Reggie Jackson hit three consecutive home runs**
> **in game six, 1977**

I think there are going to be a lot of Reggies born in this town.

> **Bill Lee, Boston Red Sox pitcher,**
> **after Jackson's performance in game six, 1977**

Reggie Jackson . . . he could have won an Oscar. He had to settle for the MVP Award.

Art Spander, *San Francisco Examiner*, 1981

1978: New York Yankees vs. Los Angeles Dodgers

Something odd always happens around him.

Bob Lemon, New York Yankees manager,
after Reggie Jackson deflected a thrown ball with his hip
in a key play in the Series, 1978

We saw our strengths in the World Series. Here came the El Lay Nice Guys. And waiting for the Dodgers were the meanest pack of bastards who ever pulled on pinstripes, playing in the meanest section of town.

Pete Hamill, *New York Daily News*, 1978

1981: Los Angeles Dodgers vs. New York Yankees

If you're the straw that stirs the drink, why don't you give Winfield a sip?

Reggie Jackson, New York Yankees outfielder,
quoting a fan's telegram on Dave Winfield's slump, 1981

They left four days later like Napoleon's troops retreating from Moscow. Napoleon's troops may have left more equipment behind, but George's left more men on base.

Ed Linn, *Steinbrenner's Yankees*, 1982

Selected Bibliography

Allen, Lee. *The American League Story*. New York: Hill and Wang, 1962.

———. *The National League Story*. New York: Hill and Wang, 1961.

———. *The World Series*. New York: G. P. Putnam's Sons, 1969.

Allen, Maury. *Big-Time Baseball*. New York: Hart, 1978.

———. *Mr. October*. New York: Times Books, 1981.

———. *Where Have You Gone, Joe DiMaggio?* New York: E. P. Dutton, 1975.

Allen, Maury, with Bo Belinsky. *Bo: Pitching and Wooing*. New York: Dial, 1973.

Anderson, Dave; Chass, Murray; Creamer, Robert; and Rosenthal, Harold. *The Yankees*. New York: Random House, 1979.

Angell, Roger. *Five Seasons*. New York: Simon and Schuster, 1977.

———. *Late Innings*. New York: Simon and Schuster, 1982.

———. *The Summer Game*. New York: Simon and Schuster, 1972.

Asinof, Eliot. *Eight Men Out*. New York: Holt, Rinehart and Winston, 1963.

Barber, Red, and Creamer, Bob. *Rhubarb in the Catbird Seat*. Garden City, N.Y.: Doubleday, 1968.

Bench, Johnny, and Brashler, William. *Catch You Later*. New York: Harper & Row, 1979.

Boswell, Thomas. *How Life Imitates the World Series*. Garden City, N.Y.: Doubleday, 1982.

Bouton, Jim. *Ball Four*. Edited by Leonard Shecter. New York: World, 1970.

———. *I'm Glad You Didn't Take It Personally*. New York: William Morrow, 1971.

Breslin, Jimmy. *Can't Anybody Here Play This Game?*. New York: Viking, 1963.

Brosnan, Jim. *The Long Season*. New York: Harper & Row, 1960.

———. *Pennant Race*. New York: Harper & Row, 1962.

Cobb, Tyrus, with Al Stump. *My Life in Baseball*. Garden City, N.Y.: Doubleday, 1961.

Creamer, Robert W. *Babe*. New York. Simon and Schuster, 1974.

Daley, Arthur. *Kings of the Home Run*. New York: G. P. Putnam's Sons, 1962.

Danzig, Allison, and Reichler, Joe. *The History of Baseball*. New York: Prentice-Hall, 1959.

De Gregorio, George. *Joe DiMaggio*. New York: Stein and Day, 1981.

Dickey, Glenn. *The History of American League Baseball*. New York: Stein and Day, 1980.

———. *The History of National League Baseball*. New York: Stein and Day, 1979.

Durocher, Leo, with Ed Linn. *Nice Guys Finish Last*. New York: Simon and Schuster, 1975.

Durso, Joseph. *Casey*. Englewood Cliffs, N.J.: Prentice-Hall, 1967.

Einstein, Charles. *Willie's Time*. New York: J. B. Lippincott, 1979.

Einstein, Charles, ed. *The Fireside Book of Baseball*. New York: Simon and Schuster, 1956.

———. *The Second Fireside Book of Baseball*. New York: Simon and Schuster, 1962.

———. *The Third Fireside Book of Baseball*. New York: Simon and Schuster, 1968.

Enright, Jim. *The Chicago Cubs*. New York: Rutledge, 1975.

Flood, Curt, with Richard Carter. *The Way It Is*. New York: Trident, 1971.

Ford, Whitey; Mantle, Mickey; and Durso, Joseph. *Whitey and Mickey*. New York: Viking, 1977.

Frick, Ford C. *Games, Asterisks, and People*. New York: Crown, 1973.

Garagiola, Joe. *Baseball Is a Funny Game*. New York: J. B. Lippincott, 1960.

Gerlach, Larry R. *The Men in Blue*. New York: Viking, 1980.

Hano, Arnold. *A Day in the Bleachers*. New York: Thomas Y. Crowell, 1955.

Hertzel, Bob. *The Big Red Machine*. Englewood Cliffs, N.J.: Prentice-Hall, 1976.

Hill, Art. *I Don't Care If I Never Come Back*. New York: Simon and Schuster, 1980.

Holmes, Tommy. *The Dodgers*. New York: Rutledge, 1975.

Holtzman, Jerome, ed. *Fielder's Choice*. New York: Harcourt Brace Jovanovich, 1980.

Honig, Donald. *The October Heroes*. New York: Simon and Schuster, 1979.

Hood, Robert. *The Gashouse Gang*. New York: William Morrow, 1975.

Hornsby, Rogers. *My War with Baseball*. New York: Coward-McCann, 1962.

Houk, Ralph G. *Ballplayers Are Human, Too*. Edited by Charles Dexter. New York: G. P. Putnam's Sons, 1962.

Jackson, Reggie. *Reggie*. Chicago: Playboy Press, 1975.

Jacobson, Steve. *The Best Team Money Can Buy*. New York: Atheneum, 1978.

Jordan, Pat. *A False Spring*. New York: Dodd, Mead, 1975.

————. *The Suitors of Spring*. New York: Dodd, Mead, 1973.

Kahn, Roger. *The Boys of Summer*. New York: Harper & Row, 1973.

————. *A Season in the Sun*. New York: Harper & Row, 1977.

Kerrane, Kevin, and Grossinger, Richard, eds. *Baseball Diamonds*. New York: Anchor, 1980.

Koppett, Leonard. *The New York Mets*. New York: Macmillan, 1970.

————. *A Thinking Man's Guide to Baseball*. New York: E. P. Dutton, 1967.

Koufax, Sandy, and Linn, Ed. *Koufax*. New York: Viking, 1966.

Lieb, Fred. *Baseball As I Have Known It*. New York: Coward, McCann & Geoghegan, 1977.

Luciano, Ron, and Fisher, Dave. *The Umpire Strikes Back*. New York: Bantam, 1982.

Lyle, Sparky, and Golenbock, Peter. *The Bronx Zoo*. New York: Crown, 1979.

McCallum, John D. *Ty Cobb*. New York: Praeger, 1975.

McGraw, Tug and Durso, Joseph. *Screwball*. Boston: Houghton Mifflin, 1974.

Mead, William B. *Even the Browns*. Chicago: Contemporary Books, 1978.

Michelson, Herbert. *Charlie O*. New York: Bobbs-Merrill, 1975.

Mosedale, John. *The Greatest of All.* New York: Dial, 1974.

Okrent, Daniel, and Lewine, Harris, eds. *The Ultimate Baseball Book.* Boston: Houghton Mifflin, 1979.

Paige, Leroy (Satchel), with David Lipman. *Maybe I'll Pitch Forever.* Garden City, N.Y.: Doubleday, 1962.

Parrott, Harold. *The Lords of Baseball.* New York: Praeger, 1976.

Pepe, Phil. *The Wit and Wisdom of Yogi Berra.* New York: Hawthorn, 1974.

Perry, Gaylord, and Sudyk, Ed. *Me and the Spitter.* New York: E. P. Dutton, 1974.

Peterson, Harold. *The Man Who Invented Baseball.* New York: Charles Scribner's Sons, 1973.

Peterson, Robert W. *Only the Ball Was White.* Englewood Cliffs, N.J.: Prentice-Hall, 1970.

Plimpton, George. *One for the Record.* New York: Harper & Row, 1974.

————. *Out of My League.* New York: Harper & Row, 1961.

Rice, Damon. *Seasons Past.* New York: Praeger, 1976.

Reichler, Joe, ed. *The Game and the Glory.* Englewood Cliffs, N.J.: Prentice-Hall, 1976.

Rickey, Branch. *The American Diamond.* New York: Simon and Schuster, 1965.

Ritter, Lawrence S. *The Glory of Their Times.* New York: Macmillan, 1966.

Robinson, Jackie, and Duckett, Alfred. *Breakthrough to the Big Leagues.* New York: Harper & Row, 1965.

Roseboro, John, and Libby, Bill. *Glory Days with the Dodgers.* New York: Atheneum, 1978.

Rust, Art Jr. *Get That Nigger Off the Field.* New York: Delacorte, 1976.

Ruth, Babe, and Considine, Bob. *The Babe Ruth Story.* New York: E. P. Dutton, 1948.

Schoor, Gene. *Billy Martin.* Garden City, N.Y.: Doubleday, 1980.

Seymour, Harold. *Baseball.* New York: Oxford University Press, 1960.

Smith, Curt. *America's Dizzy Dean.* St. Louis: Bethany, 1978.

Smith, Robert. *Babe Ruth's America.* New York: Thomas Y. Crowell, 1974.

————. *Baseball.* New York: Simon and Schuster, 1970.

Thompson, Fresco, with Cy Rice. *Every Diamond Doesn't Sparkle.* New York: David McKay, 1964.

Uecker, Bob, with Mickey Herskowitz. *Catcher in the Wry.* New York: G. P. Putnam's Sons, 1982.

Vecsey, George. *Joy in Mudville*. New York: McCall, 1970.

Veeck, Bill, with Ed Linn. *The Hustler's Handbook*. New York: G. P. Putnam's Sons, 1965.

————. *Veeck as in Wreck*. New York: G. P. Putnam's Sons, 1962.

Voight, David Quentin. *American Baseball*. Norman, Okla.: University of Oklahoma Press, 1966.

Wallop, Douglas. *The Year the Yankees Lost the Pennant*. New York: Frank Music Co., 1957.

Weaver, Earl. *Winning!* New York: William Morrow, 1972.

Williams, Ted, and Underwood, John. *My Turn at Bat*. New York: Simon and Schuster, 1969.

Index

Aaron, Henry, 72, 93, 101, 130, 188, 191
Ace, Goodman, 90
Ackerman, Al, 108
Adams, Franklin P., 86
Alexander, Grover Cleveland, 151
Algren, Nelson, 223
Allen, Lee, 88, 90
Allen, Maury, 81, 196
Allen, Mel, 202
Allen, Richie, 81, 121, 172
Allen, Woody, 12
Alston, Walter, 107
Anderson, Shirlee, 220
Anderson, Sparky, 30, 93, 107, 122, 150, 213, 226
Angell, Roger, 4, 23, 32, 53, 63, 85, 133, 139, 148, 160
Appling, Luke, 81
Ashburn, Richie, 31, 36, 169, 182
Ashby, Alan, 75
Asinof, Eliot, 229
Augustine, Jerry, 156
Axthelm, Peter, 134

Babitz, Eve, 9
Baer, Arthur, 11, 40, 47, 97, 117, 132, 167, 218
Bailey, Ed, 110
Baker, Russell, 123
Bamberger, George, 173, 191, 193
Bando, Sal, 38, 148
Banks, Ernie, 82, 119
Bannister, Alan, 84
Barber, Red, 202
Barber, Steve, 161
Barker, Len, 161
Barney, Rex, 92, 161
Barnicle, Mike, 25
Barrow, Ed, 57
Barzun, Jacques, 3, 21, 117, 221
Bates, Elmer E., 61
Bavasi, Buzzie, 33, 41, 132, 142, 150, 211
Beard, Gordon, 92
Belanger, Mark, 12, 209
Belinsky, Bo, 33, 39, 101, 119, 149, 161, 186, 199
Bell, Cool Papa, 14, 131

Bell, Marty, 30, 120, 196
Bench, Johnny, 51, 91, 219
Benchley, Robert, 62
Bender, Chief, 13
Benedict, Bruce, 192
Bengough, Benny, 16
Berg, Moe, 82, 131
Bergman, Dave, 79
Berra, Yogi, 3, 17, 19, 38, 62, 68, 72, 82, 100, 105, 119, 139, 154, 155, 158, 169, 176, 179, 184, 225
Billingham, Jack, 130
Bisher, Furman, 177, 199
Blackwell, Tim, 12
Blasingame, Don, 158
Blefary, Curt, 221
Blue, Vida, 108, 163, 203
Blyleven, Burt, 22
Bodie, Ping, 141
Boggs, Tommy, 160
Bolin, Bob, 173
Bonds, Bobby, 14, 53, 176
Bonham, Tiny, 60
Bordagary, French, 131
Bosetti, Rick, 43
Boswell, Thomas, 7, 10, 26, 42, 63, 76, 106, 136, 167, 183, 188, 192, 200, 216, 222
Boudreau, Lou, 83, 144
Bouton, Jim, 17, 18, 43, 45, 49, 50, 82, 101, 109, 113, 118, 120, 122, 141, 149, 159, 160, 163, 165, 176, 183, 186, 187, 210, 212
Bouton, Mike, 220
Bouton, Paula, 104
Boyer, Clete, 138
Brabender, Gene, 104
Branca, Ralph, 78
Brashler, William, 63
Breslin, Jimmy, 95, 142, 180
Bressler, Rube, 132, 142
Brett, George, 57, 69, 70, 83, 92
Brett, Ken, 28, 156
Brewer, Chet, 87
Bricker, Charles, 43, 133
Brickhouse, Jack, 225
Bridges, Rocky, 18, 30, 49, 55, 68, 74, 101, 106, 119, 133, 144, 154, 212
Brinkley, David, 29
Brock, Lou, 12, 131, 154

Broeg, Bob, 142
Brookens, Tom, 70
Brooks, Albert, 64
Brosnan, Jim, 28, 30, 45, 127, 162, 195
Broun, Heywood, 110, 168, 189
Brown, Bobby, 72, 83
Brown, Gates, 31, 74
Brown, Warren, 186, 223
Buck, Jack, 151
Burdette, Lew, 162, 189
Burgess, Smokey, 56
Burke, Michael, 147
Burleson, Rick, 84
Burns, George, 37
Burns, William, 162
Busby, Steve, 217

Cabell, Enos, 213
Caen, Herb, 6, 42
Camilli, Dolph, 84
Camilli, Lou, 30
Campanella, Roy, 4, 22, 27
Cannizzaro, Chris, 84
Cannon, Jimmy, 14, 72, 132, 142, 146, 167, 195
Caray, Harry, 155, 199
Carew, Rod, 84
Carlin, George, 9
Carlton, Steve, 162, 202
Carner, JoAnne, 112
Carroll, Clay, 162
Carson, Johnny, 29, 33, 112, 149, 180, 203, 204
Cartwright, Alexander, 157
Cash, Norm, 53
Cater, Danny, 41
Catton, Bruce, 63
Cepeda, Orlando, 164
Chance, Dean, 159, 190
Chandler, Raymond, 132, 158
Chapman, Ray, 60, 169
Charboneau, Joe, 75, 120
Chartoff, Melanie, 40
Cheever, John, 25, 69
Chylak, Nestor, 210
Cicotte, Eddie, 222
Ciensczyk, Frank, 149
Clark, Al, 108
Clark, Justice Tom, 12
Clemente, Roberto, 60

Clyde, David, 214
Coates, Jim, 163, 225
Cobb, Ty, 11, 52, 71, 84, 86, 96, 131, 141, 146, 179, 206, 216
Cohn, Lowell, 43, 102, 111, 210
Cole, Dave, 39
Coleman, Choo Choo, 84
Coleman, Jerry, 137, 165, 203
Collins, Dave, 70
Collins, Eddie, 144
Coniff, Frank, 42
Conlan, Jocko, 132
Connors, Chuck, 150
Conroy, Pat, 183
Cooke, Bob, 161
Cooper, Walker, 218
Cope, Myron, 133
Cosell, Howard, 119
Cousins, Norman, 65
Coveleski, Stanley, 215
Covington, Wes, 73
Cox, Billy, 84
Craig, Roger, 163
Crawford, Sam, 177
Creamer, Robert W., 25
Crouse, Buck, 16
Cuellar, Mike, 163
Cummins, Martha, 98
Curtis, John, 6

Dahlgren, Babe, 84
Daley, Arthur, 182
Daley, Steve, 28
Dark, Alvin, 42, 64, 108, 165, 170, 196
Davis, Willie, 132
Dawson, Andre, 129
Dawson, Ted, 152
Dean, Dizzy, 11, 16, 17, 30, 54, 95, 126, 139, 146, 153, 164, 168, 172, 179, 182, 189, 194, 201, 208
DeMars, Billy, 94
Dickey, Bill, 21
Dickey, Glenn, 49, 65
Dickson, Paul, 53
DiMaggio, Joe, 35, 127, 132, 182, 218
Donatelli, Augie, 208
Downey, Joan, 112
Downing, Al, 164

Doyle, Larry, 34
Drabowsky, Moe, 164
Drebinger, John, 59, 141
Dreesen, Tom, 29
Dressen, Charlie, 105
Dryden, Charles, 44
Drysdale, Don, 128, 164, 168, 192, 203
Dugan, Joe, 35, 185
Duren, Ryne, 165
Durning, Charles, 114
Durocher, Leo, 4, 13, 30, 50, 77, 82, 84, 89, 91, 108, 109, 122, 138, 139, 140, 150, 164, 207, 209, 216
Durso, Joseph, 171
Dutiel, H. J., 4
Dykes, Jimmy, 11, 39, 82, 169, 208

Edler, Dave, 70
Egan, Dave, 114
Einhorn, Eddie, 29
Einstein, Charles, 5, 51
Eisenhardt, Roy, 99
Eisenhower, Dwight D., 179
Engle, Joe, 146
Epstein, Mike, 133, 154
Erskine, Carl, 139
Eskow, John, 6, 196
Espinosa, Nino, 217
Essian, Jim, 79
Estrada, Chuck, 46
Etten, Nick, 84
Evans, Dwight, 76
Evers, Johnny, 194

Face, Elroy, 190
Fairly, Ron, 12, 78
Fallon, William J., 223
Farrell, James T., 64
Feather, William, 63
Feller, Bob, 107, 121, 128, 165
Ferrara, Al, 63
Fetzer, John, 31
Fidrych, Mark, 18, 50, 97, 128, 155, 188
Figueroa, Ed, 123
Fimrite, Ron, 221
Fingers, Rollie, 165
Finley, Charles O., 38, 70, 148, 149, 154, 155, 196, 213

Fisk, Carlton, 57, 145
Fitzgerald, Ray, 4, 222
Flanagan, Mike, 37, 173
Fletcher, Art, 166
Flood, Curt, 14, 50, 97
Ford, Gerald R., 180
Ford, Whitey, 48, 82, 137, 163, 191
Forman, Al, 208
Foster, George, 53, 133, 134, 156
Fowler, Art, 46, 55, 143, 160
Fox, Larry, 147
Foxx, Jimmy, 84
Foytack, Paul, 190
Frank, Stanley, 83
Franks, Herman, 29
Frazee, Harry, 58
Freese, Gene, 212
Frey, Jim, 83, 109
Frick, Ford C., 58, 149
Frisch, Frankie, 41, 67, 202
Fuentes, Tito, 219
Fullerton, Hugh, 222
Furillo, Carl, 55, 127

Gallico, Paul, 4, 44
Gamble, Oscar, 75, 82, 134
Gammons, Peter, 196
Garagiola, Joe, 12, 28, 41, 83, 84, 90, 91, 110, 116, 129, 140, 158, 159, 188, 192, 208, 213, 216
Garcia, Dave, 98
Garner, Phil, 32
Garvey, Cynthia, 86
Garvey, Steve, 65, 85, 110, 164, 199, 226
Gehrig, Lou, 86
Gehringer, Charlie, 87
Geiberger, Al, 129
Gent, Peter, 18
Gerstle, Philip, 9
Giamatti, A. Bartlett, 5, 147, 213, 226
Gibson, Bob, 165, 166
Gibson, Josh, 77, 87, 117, 131
Giles, Warren, 208
Gilman, Richard, 123
Goetz, Larry, 208
Goldwyn, Samuel, 127
Gomez, Lefty, 56, 74, 85, 86, 87, 133, 138, 153, 166, 186, 187

Goosen, Greg, 87
Gordon, Sid, 40
Gorman, Tom, 208
Gosger, Jim, 118
Gossage, Goose, 166
Graham, Frank, 141, 223
Grant, M. Donald, 128
Grant, Mudcat, 14
Green, Gene, 22, 162
Greenberg, Hank, 195
Greenwald, Hank, 24, 32, 38, 41, 43, 69, 76, 98, 129, 160, 204, 210, 214
Gregg, Eric, 15, 57
Gregory, Dick, 14
Grich, Bobby, 90
Griffith, Calvin, 34
Griffith, Clark, 58
Grimsley, Ross, 167
Groh, Heinie, 183
Grossinger, Richard, 7
Grote, Jerry, 219
Grove, Lefty, 167
Guidry, Ron, 112, 167
Gumbel, Bryant, 9
Guthrie, Bill, 206

Haag, Irv, 176
Haddix, Harvey, 138
Haggerty, Rube, 50
Halberstam, David, 9
Hall, Donald, 5, 122
Haller, Tom, 190
Hamill, Pete, 7, 27, 180, 200, 227
Hamlin, Luke, 167
Haney, Fred, 109, 162
Hanyzewski, Ed, 168
Hargrove, Mike, 87
Harnett, Gabby, 168
Harper, Tommy, 159, 195
Harrelson, Ken, 69, 101, 141
Harris, Bucky, 158, 165
Harris, Mark, 215
Harris, Mickey, 144
Harvey, Doug, 209
Healy, Fran, 136
Hearn, Gerry, 175
Hegan, Mike, 219
Helms, Tommy, 162
Hemond, Roland, 213
Hendricks, Elrod, 163

Henrich, Tommy, 67
Herman, Babe, 68, 134
Herman, Billy, 25
Herzog, Whitey, 33, 41, 95, 169
Higbe, Kirby, 127
Higgins, George V., 26
Hill, Art, 65, 176
Hiller, Chuck, 68
Hoagland, Edward, 5, 188
Hodges, Gil, 86, 138
Hodges, Russ, 35
Hoffa, Jimmy, 163
Hoffman, Abbie, 140
Hofheinz, Judge Roy, 32
Holliday, Bug, 125
Holmes, Tommy, 142
Holtzman, Ken, 84
Hoover, Herbert C., 8, 178
Hope, Bob, 24
Horner, Bob, 88
Hornsby, Rogers, 16, 40, 62, 88, 100, 103, 137
Houk, Ralph, 180
House, Tom, 183
Hovley, Steve, 159, 212
Howard, Elston, 88
Howard, Frank, 106, 134
Howe, Steve, 57
Hoyt, Waite, 35, 142, 168
Hrabosky, Al, 159
Hubbard, Cal, 207
Hubbard, Kin, 62
Hubbell, Carl, 168, 193
Huggins, Miller, 71
Hulbert, William A., 28
Hundley, Randy, 88
Hunt, Ron, 73
Hunter, Catfish, 135, 155, 217
Hurdle, Clint, 70, 83, 93, 186
Hurst, Tim, 206
Hutchinson, Fred, 109, 110, 164

Isaminger, Jimmy, 147
Ivie, Mike, 88
Izenberg, Jerry, 199

Jackson, Joe, 16, 52, 222
Jackson, Reggie, 18, 37, 38, 59, 63, 74, 79, 135, 138, 143, 148, 151, 175, 199, 222, 227
James, Bill, 26, 108, 116
Jay, Joey, 109

Jenkins, Ferguson, 88
Jennings, Hughie, 89
John, Tommy, 56, 57, 168, 193
Johnson, Alex, 78, 136
Johnson, Cliff, 75
Johnson, Darrell, 106
Johnson, Ernie, 163
Johnson, Harry, 207
Johnson, Lyndon B., 44, 180
Johnson, Walter, 168
Johnstone, Jay, 86, 136
Jones, Sam, 142
Judge, Joe, 35

Kaat, Jim, 124, 155, 160
Kahn, Roger, 10, 27, 44, 142, 216
Kalas, Harry, 136
Kanehl, Rod, 4, 73
Keeler, Wee Willie, 71
Kelleher, Mick, 79
Kelly, King, 47, 59
Kelly, Pat, 79
Kempton, Murray, 36
Kennedy, John F., 62
Keough, Matt, 19, 39, 113, 115
Killebrew, Harmon, 191
Kiner, Ralph, 77, 136
King, Jim, 164
King, Stephen, 205
Kingman, Brian, 102, 149
Kingman, Dave, 136
Kinsella, W. P., 124
Kirksey, George, 186
Kison, Bruce, 17
Kitman, Marvin, 127
Klem, Bill, 207, 215
Kluszewski, Ted, 74
Knowles, Darold, 135
Koppett, Leonard, 37, 63, 105, 110
Koufax, Sandy, 31, 169, 180, 190, 225
Kowet, Don, 219
Kroc, Ray, 41, 147
Kuenn, Harvey, 89
Kuhel, Joe, 44
Kuhn, Bowie, 5, 149

LaCock, Pete, 28
LaCorte, Frank, 88
LaGuardia, Fiorello H., 179
Lamp, Dennis, 131

Landis, Judge, 149
Lane, Frank, 34, 48, 112, 154, 212, 216
Lang, Jack, 95
Langford, Jim, 7
Lansburgh, Sidney, Jr., 184
Lardner, John, 114, 134, 144, 150
Lardner, Ring, 52, 71, 77, 125, 132, 185, 194, 201, 207
Larsen, Don, 169, 225
LaRussa, Tony, 107
Lasorda, Tom, 19, 33, 49, 53, 57, 94, 110, 156, 177, 188
Lau, Charlie, 79, 191
Lavagetto, Cookie, 118
Lee, Bill, 19, 26, 34, 37, 48, 56, 64, 65, 98, 106, 116, 119, 123, 130, 149, 170, 226
Lefebvre, Jim, 43, 123
Lemon, Bob, 6, 48, 110, 151, 160, 168, 204, 227
Lemonds, Dave, 122
Leonard, John, 9
Letterman, Dave, 204
Levant, Oscar, 132
Levine, Howard, 83
Lewis, Joe E., 35
Lewis, Sinclair, 3
Liebling, A. J., 35
Lietz, Jack, 210
Linn, Ed, 227
Linz, Phil, 53, 212
Lockhart, Mrs. Tokie, 161
Lockwood, Skip, 6, 159
Loes, Billy, 36, 126, 216, 223, 224
Lolich, Mickey, 56
Lopat, Ed, 170
Lopes, Dave, 76
Lopez, Al, 96, 175
Lowenstein, John, 75, 166, 217
Luciano, Ron, 25, 31, 109, 112, 114, 123, 136, 151, 174, 210, 219
Lumpe, Jerry, 89
Lurie, Bob, 98
Lyle, Sparky, 140, 159, 167, 196
Lyons, Ted, 82, 139

MacArthur, General Douglas, 208
McBride, Joseph, 19

McCarthy, Joe, 67, 85, 105, 194, 207, 211
McCarver, Tim, 22, 162, 165
McCatty, Steve, 38, 149
McConnell, Dorothy C., 120
McCovey, Willie, 89
McCree, Birdie, 168
McDowell, Sam, 73, 171
McGeehan, W. O., 48
McGraw, John, 67, 95, 96, 103, 110, 185, 215
McGraw, Tug, 5, 19, 40, 64, 93, 171, 185, 188, 216
MacKenzie, Ken, 127
McLain, Denny, 56
McNertney, Jerry, 84
MacPhail, Larry, 150
Mack, Connie, 39, 71, 182
Mackey, Biz, 172
Maddox, Garry, 79, 136
Madlock, Bill, 28, 75
Maglie, Sal, 170, 190
Malamud, Bernard, 5
Malzone, Frank, 89
Mantle, Mickey, 56, 101, 127, 137, 165, 177
Maranville, Rabbit, 47, 89
Marciano, Mrs., 22
Marion, Marty, 126
Maris, Roger, 42, 137
Marquard, Rube, 174
Marshall, Bob, 136, 139
Marshall, Jim, 38
Marshall, Mike, 64, 154
Martin, Billy, 49, 59, 104, 111, 112, 122, 135, 137, 151, 167, 197
Martin, Pepper, 54, 90
Martin, Renie, 170
Marx, Groucho, 35
Mathewson, Christy, 171, 185, 206
Matthews, Eddie, 103
Matthews, Wid, 155
Mauch, Gene, 7, 81, 106, 161, 173, 203, 209
May, Lee, 74
May, Milt, 11
May, Rudy, 83
Mayberry, John, 90
Mays, Willie, 14, 138, 224

Mazzilli, Lee, 69
Meany, Tom, 167
Medich, Doc, 87
Medwick, Ducky, 31
Medwick, Joe, 139
Mencken, H. L., 194
Merchant, Larry, 93
Michaels, Al, 10, 96, 203, 214
Michelson, Herb, 142
Miller, Ray, 18, 46, 199
Miller, Stu, 171
Minton, Greg, 98
Mize, Johnny, 90, 184
Mizell, Vinegar Bend, 117
Monday, Rick, 88, 94, 135
Moore, Roy, 90
Morgan, Joe, 90, 133, 141
Mosedale, John, 183
Mungo, Van Lingo, 171
Munson, Thurman, 104, 174
Murcer, Bobby, 42, 74, 76, 139, 172
Murphy, Edward T., 27, 195
Murphy, Jimmy, 195
Murray, Jim, 7, 33, 42, 68, 84, 89, 93, 107, 118, 129, 138, 147, 148, 187, 199, 222
Musial, Stan, 72, 139, 147, 175, 190, 202

Nabors, Jack, 39
Nahorodny, Bill, 213
Nelson, Lindsey, 10, 33, 96, 116, 175, 184, 192, 204
Nettles, Graig, 12, 37, 90, 151
Neudecker, Jerry, 209
Newhouser, Hal, 82
Niekro, Phil, 172
North, Bill, 107
Nunn, Howie, 55

Oberkfell, Ken, 41
Oceak, Frank, 121
O'Doul, Lefty, 190
Ogden, Sam, 216
O'Malley, Walter, 195
Osteen, Claude, 212
Otis, Amos, 209
Ott, Ed, 133
Ott, Mel, 62, 82

Owens, Jim, 32, 45
Oyler, Ray, 50
Ozark, Danny, 136

Paciorek, Tom, 166
Pagliaroni, Jim, 48, 49, 219
Paige, Satchel, 7, 21, 50, 55, 87, 126, 131, 153, 172, 187, 218
Palmer, Jim, 56, 107, 115, 173
Park, Gary, 33
Parker, Dan, 150
Parrott, Harold, 109, 150
Patek, Fred, 119
Paul, Gabe, 161, 167, 173
Pegler, Westbrook, 52
Pepitone, Joe, 32, 62, 91
Perez, Tony, 91
Perkins, Broderick, 204
Perry, Allison, 220
Perry, Gaylord, 46, 53, 155, 173, 191
Pesky, Johnny, 37
Peters, Hank, 213
Peterson, Harold, 5
Phair, George, 39
Phillips, B. J., 112, 200
Piersall, Jimmy, 29, 114, 140, 148
Piniella, Lou, 56, 140
Pipp, Wally, 54
Plimpton, George, 10, 159
Popovich, Paul, 91
Povich, Shirley, 169, 224
Powell, Boog, 91
Pride, Charley, 14
Prince, Bob, 140, 202

Quinn, Jack, 119, 174
Quisenberry, Dan, 19, 79, 99, 156, 160, 170, 192

Rader, Doug, 107
Randle, Lenny, 53
Raschi, Vic, 21, 92
Raymond, Bugs, 174
Reardon, Beans, 207
Reddicliffe, Steven, 152
Reichardt, Rich, 140
Reiser, Pete, 54, 135
Remy, Jerry, 92
Reston, James, 180

Revering, Dave, 38
Reynolds, Quentin, 113
Reza, H. G., 176
Rhodes, Dusty, 140, 171, 224
Rice, Grantland, 110
Rice, Jim, 141
Rice, Johnny, 208
Richards, Paul, 105, 161, 164
Richardson, Bobby, 92
Richler, Mordecai, 26
Rickey, Branch, 4, 13, 67, 72, 93, 100, 108, 131, 138, 150, 153, 177, 179, 186, 211
Rickles, Don, 18, 85
Ritz, David, 27, 181
Rivers, Mickey, 135, 156
Rixey, Eppa, 157
Rizzuto, Phil, 92, 140, 184, 203, 204
Robinson, Arthur, 35
Robinson, Brooks, 92
Robinson, Frank, 14, 57, 113, 141
Robinson, Jackie, 93, 156
Roe, Preacher, 157, 158
Rogell, William, 164
Rogers, Steve, 174
Rogers, Will, 178, 197, 221
Rogovin, Saul, 158
Rooker, Jim, 51
Rooney, Andy, 184
Roosevelt, Franklin D., 179
Rose, Karolyn, 220
Rose, Pete, 14, 40, 59, 73, 91, 92, 93, 94, 101, 122, 128, 134, 191, 217, 226
Rose, Petie, 220
Rosen, Al, 78, 104
Rosenblatt, Roger, 6
Rosenthal, Harold, 100
Roth, Mark, 61
Rowswell, Rosey, 201
Royko, Mike, 28, 38, 98, 143, 144, 177
Rudi, Joe, 167
Ruiz, Chico, 212
Runyon, Damon, 29, 171
Ruppert, Jacob, 168
Russell, Bill, 90
Ruth, Babe, 49, 54, 59, 61, 72, 77, 100, 126, 141, 178, 186
Ryan, Nolan, 174

Sain, Johnny, 56, 123, 127, 155, 174
Sanguillen, Manny, 94
Sax, Steve, 94
Schaap, Dick, 38, 136
Scheinblum, Richie, 30
Schmidt, Mike, 7, 94
Schoendienst, Red, 106
Schulian, John, 112
Schultz, Joe, 50, 73, 113
Scully, Vin, 12, 188
Seaver, Tom, 36, 175, 226
Sewell, Rip, 189
Shafer, Robert, 78
Shah, Diane K., 112
Shapiro, Leonard, 7
Sharon, Dick, 174
Shaw, Bob, 175
Shaw, George Bernard, 8
Shea, Thomas P., 162
Shecter, Leonard, 106, 137, 196
Sheed, Wilfrid, 183
Sheehan, Tom, 42
Shepherd, Jean, 28
Sherrod, Blackie, 84
Sherry, Larry, 174
Shirley, Bob, 42
Shor, Toots, 36, 48
Short, Bob, 115, 154
Siebert, Dick, 51
Simmons, Curt, 130
Simmons, Lon, 19, 20, 31, 33, 34, 57, 64, 66, 91, 92, 115, 143, 165, 170, 203, 205, 210
Simmons, Ted, 12, 94
Sims, Duke, 135
Skowron, Moose, 94
Slaughter, Enos, 150
Smith, Mayo, 118
Smith, Ozzie, 42
Smith, Red, 3, 78, 146, 148
Smith, Reggie, 37, 69
Smith, Ron, 134, 171
Spahn, Warren, 78, 114, 140, 175
Spander, Art, 227
Speaker, Tris, 131
Stallard, Tracy, 176, 202
Stanhouse, Don, 110, 176
Stanky, Eddie, 94, 126, 144
Stanley, Fred, 83
Stargell, Willie, 6, 93, 162, 191

Steinbeck, John, 44
Steinberg, David, 118
Steinbrenner, George, 59, 69, 104, 129, 151, 166
Stello, Dick, 209
Stengel, Casey, 17, 22, 27, 32, 36, 48, 49, 55, 62, 68, 72, 83, 84, 85, 87, 88, 89, 92, 94, 95, 103, 111, 113, 121, 125, 137, 153, 154, 158, 163, 165, 170, 171, 172, 174, 176, 183, 187, 198, 202, 211, 215, 218, 223, 224
Stephenson, Jerry, 4
Stevens, Bob, 138
Stieb, Dave, 160
Stone, Steve, 188
Stoneham, Horace, 36
Stoneman, Bill, 36, 128
Stuart, Dick, 52, 68
Sukeforth, Clyde, 78
Sullivan, Frank, 68, 212
Sundberg, Jim, 112
Sutton, Don, 32, 40, 88, 128, 169, 191, 220
Swan, Craig, 128
Swift, Bob, 59
Swift, E. M., 43
Swoboda, Ron, 73, 143
Symington, Stuart, 148

Taft, William Howard, 178
Talbot, Fred, 25, 43, 101, 176
Tanner, Chuck, 140, 156
Taylor, Ron, 17, 36
Tebbetts, Birdie, 158
Templeton, Garry, 95
Terry, Bill, 26, 95, 110
Thomas, Gorman, 143
Thompson, Fresco, 8, 26, 39, 45, 126, 134, 174, 207, 212, 219
Throneberry, Marv, 63, 95
Thurber, James, 62
Torre, Joe, 107, 166
Tramer, Bennett, 31
Trimble, Joe, 85
Trout, Dizzy, 176
Truman, Harry S., 179
Turan, Kenneth, 6
Turner, Jim, 195
Turner, Ted, 23, 51, 97, 128, 152, 156

Uecker, Bob, 19, 22, 96, 99, 172, 200, 219
Updike, John, 25, 63

Valenzuela, Fernando, 176, 217
Vaughn, Bill, 32, 65
Veeck, Bill, 9, 41, 59, 65, 85, 87, 89, 98, 122, 123, 128, 129, 144, 147, 199, 212
Vescey, George, 145
Vidal, Gore, 6
Villaneuva, Danny, 10
Virdon, Bill, 69

Waddell, Rube, 177
Wagner, Honus, 3, 96, 125
Wagner, Leon, 118
Walsh, Ed, 177
Walter, Bucky, 171
Walters, Bucky, 195
Walters, Charlie, 34
Waner, Paul, 143
Ward, Pete, 96
Washington, Claudell, 143
Watson, Bob, 217
Weaver, Earl, 9, 18, 25, 45, 64, 74, 80, 114, 115, 119, 151, 154, 163, 216
Weiss, George, 95, 224
Wendelstedt, Harry, 109, 209
Westrum, Wes, 224
White, Ernie, 143
White, Russ, 147
Whitman, Burt, 141
Wieder, Robert S., 184
Wilcox, Milt, 192
Wilcox, Frederick B., 156
Will, George, 29, 66
Williams, Billy, 75
Williams, Delores, 219
Williams, Dick, 106, 170
Williams, Edward Bennett, 148
Williams, Stan, 134
Williams, Ted, 17, 44, 101, 115, 122, 126, 143, 187, 197
Wills, Maury, 116, 183
Wilson, Bert, 202
Wilson, Earl, 118
Wilson, Flip, 118
Wilson, George, 73
Wilson, Hack, 144

Wilson, Jimmy, 189
Winfield, Dave, 41
Wolfe, Thomas, 198
Wolfe, Tom, 46
Wolff, Miles, 120
Wood, Joe, 169
Woolf, Bob, 97, 98
Wrigley, Philip K., 155
Wulf, Steve, 26
Wynn, Early, 177, 190

Yastrzemski, Carl, 74, 144, 166
Yost, Eddie, 172
Young, Cy, 131
Young, Dick, 27, 108, 129, 137, 197, 225

Ziegel, Vic, 91
Zimmer, Don, 116, 141
Zinsser, William, 63
Zisk, Richie, 43

Bob Chieger is a free-lance writer and editor who has been collecting quotations for seven years. He has worked for several magazines and publishing houses, and his own work has appeared in New West, Games, Panorama *and the* San Francisco Chronicle. *He lives in Los Gatos, California.*